Depression and the New Deal

Roger Smalley

Series Editor: Bryn O'Callaghan

The British Association for American Studies gratefully acknowledges generous assistance from the Cultural Affairs Office of the American Embassy.

Published by Longman Group UK Limited in association with the British Association for American Studies

First published 1990
Fourth impression 1994

ISBN: 0 582 26754 4

Printed in Great Britain by York Publishing Services

The Publisher's policy is to use paper manufactured from sustainable forests.

Acknowledgements

We are grateful to the following for permission to reproduce photographs:

Courtesy of the Library of Congress, Front Cover, pages 4, 9 (bottom), 16 (bottom), 28 29, 36 (bottom), 37, 38; The Hulton-Deutsch Collection, pages 1, 16 (centre), 41 (top); Brown Brothers, pages 5, 17 (top); Soil Conservation Service, page 9 (top); Courtesy Vanity Fair, copyright c 1933 (renewed 1961) by the Conde Nast Publications Inc., page 17 (second from top and bottom); Pictorial Press Limited, page 17 (third from top); Tennessee Valley Authority, page 21; *American History: A Survey*, R.N. Current et al., 1961, Alfred A. Knopf, reproduced with permission by McGraw-Hill Publication Company, page 22; Reproduced by courtesy of the Franklin D. Roosevelt Library, pages 25, 60; Chicago Historical Society, pages 34, 43; Wide World Photos Inc., page 41 (bottom); the *Philadelphia Enquirer*, page 42; the *Washington Post*, page 45; Fitzpatrick in the *St. Louis Post-Dispatch*, pages 48, 50 (bottom).

We apologise for the fact that although every effort has been made to trace the copyright holders for pages, 6, 7, 16 (top), 20, 26, 30, 36 (top), 41 (centre), 46, 55, 56, we have been unable to do so.

Contents

Hoover and Roosevelt: The Start of the Depression

The Depression is the name given to the period in the 1930s in which the United States' economy collapsed. During the Depression millions of people found themselves without work and living in poverty. Herbert Hoover was the Republican President during the first part of this period, from 1929 to 1933.

The New Deal is the name given to the attempts to overcome the Depression made by Franklin Roosevelt after he succeeded Hoover to become the new Democratic President in 1933.

Herbert Hoover

This orphaned farm boy from Iowa made a fortune as a mining engineer before the First World War. He subsequently became a politician and during the war was responsible for organising relief for the Belgians.

Once the United States entered the war he became War Food Administrator. In the 1920s Hoover was Secretary of Commerce and gained a reputation as being the man mainly responsible for the United States' prosperity at that time. In 1928 Hoover stood for election as President and won an easy victory over the Democratic candidate Alfred Smith.

Franklin Roosevelt

Roosevelt came from a wealthy New York family. He stood unsuccessfully as the vice-presidential candidate for the Democratic Party in the 1920 elections. The following year he contracted polio, a disease which paralysed his legs.

In 1928 Roosevelt was elected Governor of New York State and went on to establish the Temporary Emergency Relief Administration to distribute unemployment relief there. Roosevelt became the Democratic Party's presidential candidate in 1932. He won a landslide victory over Hoover and remained President until his death in 1945. Roosevelt's middle name was Delano and he is often referred to simply as 'FDR'.

The causes of the Depression

> Why when the stock crash came did the man in black silk pajamas let himself headfirst off a fire escape down ten floors to a stone sidewalk? His sixty million dollars had shrunk to ten million and he didn't see how he could get along.
> **Source 1A:** From section 23 of 'The People, Yes', published by the poet Carl Sandburg in 1936.

The Depression started in 1929, but it was caused by events which occurred throughout the 1920s.

Overproduction

During the 1920s wages for industrial workers rose by 40 per cent. More jobs became available in new industries such as car manufacturing, aviation, the manufacture of electrical goods, movies (the first talking picture was produced in 1927) and advertising.

This increase in both wage levels and jobs coincided with the introduction of hire purchase schemes, which enabled buyers to pay for goods by instalments over a given period. The result of such schemes was an increase in the demand for new consumer goods, especially cars, radios, washing machines and refrigerators, by people who could not otherwise have afforded them.

However, by 1929 the mass production of consumer goods began to outstrip demand. People were not buying goods as quickly as they were being made, and demand fell. This caused the producers of such goods to reduce wages, lay off workers, or even go out of business.

The problem of overproduction was not restricted to industry; farmers too were affected. During the First World War the American government had encouraged farmers to produce as much as possible in order to help feed the warring countries of Europe and the American forces. When the war ended demand for farm produce fell, but farmers did not cut back on production. During the 1920s many were growing far more than they could sell, and the prices of farm produce fell to levels below the costs of production.

With their incomes falling to as low as $89 a year, some farm owners had to sell their land, and others, who could not afford to pay their rents, were evicted. Because farmers lacked purchasing power, they could not afford to buy the consumer goods which were so abundant.

High tariffs (taxes on imports)

In 1922 the United States Congress passed the Fordney McCumber Act. This law required foreign manufacturers to pay a 30 per cent tariff, or import duty, on their goods before they were allowed to sell them in the United States. This meant that if foreign producers wanted to trade in the United States they had either to increase the price of their goods, or accept lower profits.

The Fordney McCumber Act gave American producers protection against foreign competition, but foreign governments retaliated by raising tariffs on American goods entering their countries. The situation became even worse in the early 1930s: trade between the United States and the rest of the world, which was vital for a healthy economy, fell by one third between 1929 and 1933.

The Wall Street Crash

Wall Street is the area of New York City where the American Stock Exchange is situated. *Stock* is the name given to a company's capital or value, which is divided into shares for sale. Shareholders are entitled to a proportion of the company's profits.

The prosperity of the 1920s enabled many Americans to buy stock for the first time. New stockbroking (or stock-selling) companies were formed to cater specifically for small investors. For example, Goldman Sachs, an established New York investment company, created the Blue Ridge Corporation and the Shenandoah Corporation for this purpose. By 1929, Americans had bought $250 million worth of stock through such companies, often borrowing money to do so.

This high demand for stock meant that for most of the 1920s its price stayed high. However, in September 1929 some investors noticed that company profits were showing signs of falling and sold their stock. Banks, believing that such sales would cause the price of stock to fall, demanded the repayment of loans they had made to people who wanted to buy stock. In turn, the borrowers tried to sell their stock to raise the money to repay their loans. This increased the amount of stock on sale to such a degree that much of it became worthless. By November 1929 this process had resulted in the financial ruin of large numbers of people.

> A cigar stock at the time [1929] was selling for $115 a share. The market collapsed. The $115 stock dropped to $2 and the company president jumped out of the window of his Wall Street office.
>
> **Source 1B:** From an interview given by Arthur Robertson, a young businessman during the Depression, to Studs Terkel in the 1960s. It forms part of a collection of memories of the Depression called *Hard Times* (1970).

---

1 Read Source 1A and Source 1B.

a) Explain the terms 'stock' and 'Wall Street'.

b) What does Sandburg mean by 'His sixty million dollars had shrunk to ten million'?

c) Which source is more sympathetic towards the suicide it describes? Explain your choice.

What was the United States like during the Depression?

Unemployment

In 1929 only 1.5 million people in the United States were unemployed. By 1933 this number had risen to more than 12 million – over 20 per cent of the work force. In some industrial cities the situation was much worse – 40 per cent of those wanting work in the city of Chicago could not find any.

At this time the United States had no system of unemployment benefit. Those without work therefore faced great hardship. And because they had no money to buy goods they could not help the economy to revive.

> The drowning man in the river
> answered the man on the bridge:
> 'I don't want to die,
> I'll lose my job in the molding room of
> the Malleable Iron and Castings Works.'
> And the living man on the bridge
> hotfooted to the molding room foreman
> of the Malleable Iron and Castings Works
> and got a short answer:
> 'You're ten minutes late. The man who
> pushed that fellow off the bridge
> is already on the job.'
>
> **Source 1C:** From section 37 of 'The People, Yes', published by the poet Carl Sandburg in 1936.

> Thousands of working class families have been thrown out of their homes because they can no longer pay the rent. In the streets of every large city workers are dropping, dying and dead from starvation and exposure. Every newspaper reports suicides of these workers, driven to desperation by unemployment and starvation.
>
> **Source 1D:** Part of the evidence given to a committee of Congress in 1931 by William Foster, leader of the American Communist Party.

Production and wages

During the Depression car production was cut by 80 per cent. Road and building construction fell by 92 per cent. Average hourly wages in manufacturing industry fell from 59 cents in 1926 to 44 cents in 1933. The total income of American farmers dropped from $12 billion to $5 billion per year. In 1932 farmers in the state of Iowa went on strike because the price they could obtain for their milk had dropped to 2 cents a quart.

The Destitute

In every city soup kitchens were opened to feed the starving. Source 1E shows one of the most famous, the South State Street soup kitchen in Chicago which was set up by the notorious gangster Al Capone.

Source 1E: The South State Street soup kitchen in Chicago.

Many families had to sell their homes in order to raise money to buy food and other essentials. Others had to leave rented accommodation because they could no longer afford it. They moved into makeshift shelters constructed from packing cases and corrugated iron on the outskirts of cities. The shanty towns which resulted were nicknamed 'Hoovervilles' because many people blamed their homelessness on President Hoover.

Hoovervilles were often built on rubbish dumps. In Source 1F a historian describes an incident at the Cicero Avenue Hooverville in Chicago:

> Another widow, who used to do housework and laundry but who was finally left without any work, fed herself and her fourteen-year-old son on garbage. Before she picked up the meat, she would always take off her glasses so that she would not be able to see the maggots; but it sometimes made the boy so sick to look at this offal and smell it that he could not bring himself to eat.
>
> **Source 1F:** From *The American Earthquake, A Documentary of the 20s and 30s,* by Edmund Wilson (1958).

In remote areas the problem of feeding the family was just as great, but there were no soup kitchens to go to as there were in the cities. Source 1H is an extract from a popular song, which describes the effects of the Depression on the singer's diet.

Source 1G: A Hooverville.

We have Hooverized our butter,
For milk we've only water,
And I haven't seen a steak in many a day,
As for pies, cakes and jellies,
We substitute sow bellies,
For which we work the county road each day.
Source 1H: From 'Beans, Bacon and Gravy' a popular song during the Depression.

Another historian described one solution used by a woman named Molly Jackson, who lived in the Appalachian mountains:

> . . . she walked into the local store, asked for a 24-pound sack of flour, gave it to her little boy to take it outside, then filled a sack of sugar and said to the storekeeper, 'Well, I'll see you in ninety days. I have to feed some children . . . I'll pay you, don't worry.' And when he objected, she pulled out her pistol (which, as a midwife travelling alone through the hills, she had a permit to carry) and said: 'Martin, if you try to take this grub away from me, God knows that if they electrocute me for it tomorrow, I'll shoot you six times in a minute.'

Source 1I: From *A People's History of the United States*, by Howard Zinn (1980).

The Bonus March

In the summer of 1923 12,000 unemployed men who had served as soldiers during the First World War marched to Washington to ask for bonuses (payments) they were owed for their wartime service. Congress refused to help them because the bonuses were not due until 1945. President Hoover ordered the army to destroy the marchers' camp on the mud flats of the Anacostia river and disperse them.

DEMANDS OF THE VETERANS:

BONUS

Congress to pass a bill for the immediate cash payment of the Bonus with the following provisions:

1. Congress authorize the immediate payment of the balance due on the adjusted service certificates, upon demand of those entitled to it.
2. All interest charges on certificates to cease.
3. All interest deducted from loans already made including the transportation loans advanced the Bonus Marchers to be added to the balance due.
4. Funds to be raised as follows:
   a) Surtax on industries;
   b) Inheritance tax;
   c) All funds for immediate war preparations;
   d) Reconstruction Finance Corporation funds.

DISABLED

Not a cent off the disability allowances.

Negro war veterans to be admitted in all hospitals.

Jim-crowing of Negro veterans to cease. This applies to all hospitals in the South in particular.

Veterans to have right to choose their own doctors and expense to be paid by the government.

UNEMPLOYED

House and feed all unemployed unmarried veterans as well as other unmarried unemployed without police surveillance at local government and federal government expense.

Unemployment and social insurance for all unemployed at the expense of the federal government and the employers.

————————— DETACH AND MAIL TO —————————

VETERANS CENTRAL RANK AND FILE COMMITTEE
P. O. BOX 38
NEW YORK CITY

Comrades:

Please send me more information about what to do to make the Bonus March a success.

NAME .... ADDRESS ....

CITY .... STATE ....

☐ I condemn the Hoover administration for using the troops against the veterans.

☐ I support immediate payment of the Bonus.

☐ I will support the March to Washington.

Issued by Veterans Central Rank and File Committee, P. O. Box 38, New York, N. Y.

Source 1J: A leaflet issued by the organisers of the Bonus March, setting out the Marchers' aims.

This is how a Washington newspaper described what happened:

> The offensive against the camp was launched at 10:09 by infantry-men with drawn bayonets, who hurled tear gas bombs into the crowd . . .
>
> With their horses at a walk, the Cavalry went down the steep embankment into the camp area, followed immediately by [more] infantrymen, who set fire to a number of huts after first making sure every human had been cleared out . . .
>
> The whole camp was a mass of flames by 11 o'clock . . . The great camp was destroyed last night almost to the last shelter.
>
> The Infantry went ahead with bayonets fixed, throwing tear gas bombs in place of hand grenades. The Cavalry came in at a charge, mostly relying on their mounts to scatter the veterans. Tanks were deployed and machine guns were in position, but the unarmed 'enemy' force did not require the use of the deadlier weapons . . .
>
> The women of the B.E.F. [Bonus Expeditionary Force], scores of them, with their children, sought new shelter. Some were hurried off to the Salvation Army quarters and charitable homes. One mother made a heart-tugging spectacle as she laid her small brood of three to sleep on a hard pavement. They slumbered soundly.

As the night wore on bewildered groups of the veterans carrying blanket rolls and other meager possessions, wandered about in the street in the vicinity of the burning shacks . . . Everywhere was the penetrating smell of burning cloth and unsalvaged bedding.

Ambulances clung to the edge of the conflict and carried off men with battered heads, with eyes streaming from unbearable doses of tear gas, and with all the other injuries that inevitably accompany civil disorder and its suppression.

Source 1K: *Washington Evening Star*, 29 July 1932.

Source 1L: Two of the tanks used against the Bonus Marchers.

Three days later, one member of President Hoover's cabinet commented:

Under the circumstances but two courses were left open to the President. One was to acquiesce in the violence and surrender the government to the mob. The other was to uphold law and order – and suppress the mob.

Source 1M: Comment on the Bonus March by Secretary of War Patrick Hurley, 2 August 1932.

An anonymous contemporary song writer took a different view of what had happened:

> Only two courses were open,
>   As anyone can see:
> To vindicate law and order
>   Or yield to anarchy.
> Granted! – the Chiefs of Government
>   Cannot tolerate mobs –
> But isn't it strange you never thought
>   Of giving the workless jobs?
>
> Only two courses were open –
>   When men who had fought for you
> Starved in the streets of our cities,
>   Finding no work to do –
> When in the richest of the countries
>   Babies went unfed –
> Strange it never occurred to you
>   To give the hungry bread!

Source 1N: From a contemporary song, 1932.

2 Read Source 1C.

a) What does this poem tell you about the unemployment problem in the United States during the Depression?

b) Do you think that the story it tells is true or made up? Does the answer to this question affect the value of the poem as a piece of historical evidence?

3 Read Source 1H.

a) In your own words describe the effects of the Depression on the singer's diet.

b) Who do you think he is blaming for the situation?

c) Explain the meaning of the last line of the song.

d) What do you think is the value of popular songs like this as sources of information for historians? Explain your answer.

4 Look at Source 1J. What evidence does it contain:

a) of racial discrimination in the armed forces at the time the source was written?

b) that war veterans were co-ordinating an attempt to force the government to pay the bonus?

c) that police and troops had been used against First World War veterans *before* the Bonus March took place?

5 Source 1J is an example of what is called a 'primary' source of historical evidence. The writings by historians quoted elsewhere in the chapter (Sources 1F and 1I) are known as 'secondary' sources.

a) What do you think is the difference?

b) Is either type of source likely to be more reliable than the other as evidence of what really happened in the past? Explain your answer.

c) Look again at Sources 1K, 1L, 1M and 1N. Which of these are primary sources and which are secondary?

The Dust Bowl

Between 1930 and 1936 over 20 million hectares of farm land in Kansas, Oklahoma, Texas, New Mexico and Colorado became desert. The area had once been animal grazing land, but during and since the First World War much of it had been ploughed up to grow crops. Without its covering of grass to protect it against the hot summers and fierce winds, the land turned into dust. The region subsequently became known as the 'Dust Bowl'.

A Kansas wheat farmer described one of the wind storms that created the Dust Bowl:

> The wind increases its velocity until it is blowing at forty to fifty miles an hour. The fine dirt is sweeping along like at express-train speed, and when the very sun is blotted out visibility is reduced to some fifty feet, or perhaps you cannot see at all, because the dust has blinded you.
> **Source 1O:** From *An Empire of Dust*, written in the 1930s by Lawrence Svobida.

Source 1P: Buried machinery on a Dust Bowl farm, in 1936.

The photograph in Source 1P shows how such storms could affect a farm. The year after that photograph was taken, a magazine reporter vividly described his impressions of the Dust Bowl (Source 1Q).

> The Dust Bowl is a dying land . . . I have not seen more than two automobiles on the road that parallels the railroad track for a hundred miles or more. I have seen human beings only when passing bleak villages, consisting of a few shacks. Houses empty, yards empty. I have not seen a single child in these ghost-like, pathetic villages. The few people I saw looked like a lost people living in a lost land.
>
> I do not exaggerate when I say that in this country there is now no life for miles upon miles; no human beings, no birds, no animals. Only a dull brown land with cracks showing. Hills furrowed with eroded gullies – you have seen pictures like that in ruins of lost civilizations.
> **Source 1Q:** George Greenfield in *Reader's Digest*, May 1937.

In his picture 'A Victim of the Dust Storms' (Source 1R) the artist Ben Shahn tried to show how conditions of this sort affected people's lives.

Source 1R: 'A Victim of the Dust Storms' – a lithograph by Ben Shahn, an artist employed by Roosevelt's Government to show the plight of the poor.

Migration

A great migration took place in the United States during the 1930s, as people left their homes and tried to find work in other parts of the country. In 1932 an estimated two million hobos (wandering workers) were travelling the roads and the railroads. Blacks moved from the south to northern cities hoping for work in industry.

After 1934 farmers from Oklahoma and Arkansas (known as the 'Okies' and the 'Arkies') moved to California looking for work on fruit farms. Their plight is described by John Steinbeck in his novel *The Grapes of Wrath*:

> And the dispossessed, the migrants, flowed into California, two hundred and fifty thousand, and three hundred thousand. Behind them new tractors were going on the land and the tenants were being forced off. And new waves were on the way, new waves of the dispossessed and the homeless, hard, intent, and dangerous . . .
>
> And the homeless hungry man, driving the road with his wife beside him and his thin children in the back seat, could look at the fallow fields which might produce food but not profit, and that man could know how a fallow field is a sin and unused land a crime against the thin children . . .
>
> And in the south he saw the golden oranges hanging on the trees, the little golden oranges on the dark green trees; and guards with shotguns patrolling the lines so a man might not pick an orange for a thin child, oranges to be dumped if the price was low . . .
>
> **Source 1S:** From The *Grapes of Wrath*, by John Steinbeck (1939).

Soon more people were leaving the United States than were entering it. Some Americans, despairing of finding jobs in the United States, emigrated to Europe. Amtorg, the Russian trading agency in New York received an average of 350 applications a day in the early 1930s from Americans who wanted to settle in the Soviet Union. On one occasion, Amtorg advertised for 6000 skilled workers and 100,000 people applied, including plumbers, carpenters, teachers, salesmen and an undertaker.

But most migrants looked for work elsewhere in the United States. One of them was a young folk singer named Woody Guthrie. Guthrie wrote:

> There's a whole big army of us rambling workers – call us migrants. Hundreds of thousands of people fighting against all kinds of odds to keep their little families sticking together; trickling along the highways and railroad tracks; living in dirty little shack towns, hunkered down along the malaria creeks, squatting in the wind of the dust-blown plains, and stranded like wild herds of cattle across the blistered deserts.
>
> A whole army of us. It's a big country. But we can take it. We can sing you songs so full of hard traveling, and hard sweating and hard fighting you'll get big clear blisters in the palms of your hands just listening to us.
>
> **Source 1T:** Woody Guthrie, quoted in *Brother, Can You Spare a Dime?*, by Milton Meltzer (1969).

Guthrie wrote many songs about the lives of the migrants. One was called 'Pastures of Plenty':

> It's a mighty hard row that my poor hands has hoed,
> My poor feet has traveled a hot dusty road;
> Out of your Dust Bowl and westward we rolled,
> And your deserts was hot and your mountains was cold.
>
> I worked in your orchards of peaches and prunes,
> I slept on the ground in the light of the moon;
> On the edge of the city you'll see us and then,
> We come with the dust and we go with the wind.

California, Arizona, I make all your crops,
Well, it's up north up to Oregon to gather your hops;
Dig the beets from your ground, cut the grapes from your vine,
To set on your table your light, sparkling wine.

It's always we rambled, that river and I,
All along your green valley I will work till I die;
My land I'll defend with my life if it be,
'Cause my pastures of plenty must always be free.
Source 1U: 'Pastures of Plenty' by Woody Guthrie.

Source 1V: Migrant 'Okies' heading for California on Route 66.

6 Imagine that you are a member of a farming family living in the Dust Bowl. Use Sources 1O, 1Q, 1R, 1S and 1V, together with pages 8–10 (the sections on the 'Dust Bowl' and 'Migration'), to describe your family's problems in the 1930s. You should mention:

– the location of the farm;
– the dust storms and their effects;
– the decisions made by the family in response to their predicament.

7 Look at Source 1R.

a) What do you think that the artist who drew this picture was aiming to do?

b) How does he attempt to achieve this aim?

c) Which of the other sources in the 'Dust Bowl' and 'Migration' sections come closest to matching the mood of the picture?

Self help

The Depression forced many Americans to use desperate methods to survive. Louis Adamic, a New York journalist, described an incident which occurred at a grocery store in 1932, when a group of 30 or 40 men asked for credit:

> When the clerk tells them business is for cash only, they bid him stand aside; they don't want to harm him, but they must have things to eat. They load up and depart.
>
> **Source 1W:** From *My America*, by Louis Adamic (1938).

Groups of unemployed men often prevented poor families who could not afford their rent from being evicted. They proved resourceful in providing help for themselves when the authorities did not.

In the city of Seattle, the Unemployed Citizens' League organised self-help on a large scale. The unemployed were allowed to pick unmarketable fruit and vegetables by nearby farmers, and to cut wood on scrub timberland. Food and firewood obtained in this way were exchanged with barbers who cut hair, seamstresses who mended clothes, carpenters who repaired houses and doctors who treated the sick.

In Pennsylvania teams of unemployed miners dug coal on company property and sold it in local towns below the commercial rate. Twenty thousand miners had become involved in this illegal activity by 1934, and they sold 5,000,000 tons of company coal. When the coal company took them to court local juries would not convict them and local jailors would not imprison them.

These self-help activities were important to people because of the inadequate welfare provision in the United States before 1933. The country had no national social security programme at all; government-organised pensions, health insurance, unemployment insurance and family allowances did not exist in the United States even though most West European countries had been providing some or all of these since the beginning of the century. There were some private charities and some local welfare schemes to help the needy – eleven states, for example, provided old age pensions – but usually states went to great lengths to avoid spending public money on the poor within their boundaries.

Three factors help to explain this situation. Firstly, many Americans believed that poverty was usually the fault of the poor themselves, so the poor were offered only a small amount of relief, which was grudgingly given. Secondly, Americans doubted the ability of the national government to provide solutions to poverty-related problems. They were used to decentralised government in most matters, not a centralised one like most countries in western Europe. Finally, during the years of prosperity in the 1920s, efforts to expand welfare services had seemed unnecessary and irrelevant to most Americans.

9 Imagine that you are involved in the incident described in Source 1W. Write out, or improvise, the conversation that takes place between members of the group and the grocery store clerk.

10 Think about why so little official help was available for people in need at the start of the Depression in the United States. Then write *two* letters to a newspaper. In your first letter try to convince your readers that the official policies are correct; in your second letter try to show that the policies are mistaken.

Hoover's attempts to deal with the Depression

Hoover became President at the end of a decade of prosperity in the United States. In the 1920s unemployment had fallen to 3 per cent and wages had increased on average by 40 per cent.

Hoover believed that this had been achieved because of the American tradition of individualism, and because of the willingness of government, employers and workers to co-operate voluntarily to create prosperity. He was so confident that the prosperity would continue that he made this claim in a speech in New York on 22 October 1928:

> Our American experiment in human welfare has yielded a degree of well-being unparalleled in all the world. It has come nearer to the abolition of poverty, to the abolition of fear of want, than humanity has ever reached before.

Source 1X: From a speech by President Hoover, 22 October 1928.

When the Depression began in 1929 Hoover was sure that the formula of hard work and minimum interference from government which had worked so well in the past would soon restore prosperity. However, as the economic situation deteriorated he realised that the government would have to do something to provide relief for the poor and encouragement for business and industry. The ways in which he tried to do this are described below.

1 His administration set up a Farm Board, whose job was to keep the prices of farm produce steady. It tried to do this by buying surplus farm produce at the commercial rate. However, by 1932 the Farm Board had spent its budget of $500 million and grain prices fell again.

Hoover had made two mistakes. He had not given the Farm Board a big enough budget, and he had not introduced laws to cut surpluses by reducing production. His efforts to persuade farmers to reduce production voluntarily went unheeded. President Roosevelt avoided making the same mistakes in 1933 when he tackled the problem of poverty amongst farmers in his Agricultural Adjustment Act (see page 23).

2 Tariffs (import duties) were increased. In 1930 Hoover signed the Hawley-Smoot Act. This law increased by 50 per cent the tariffs on 1000 farm products and manufactured goods imported from foreign countries. The new law had a similar effect to the 1922 Fordney McCumber Act (see page 2). Foreign countries retaliated by raising tariffs on American goods entering their countries, and trade fell.

Again, Roosevelt learned from the mistake. He realised that high tariffs prevented economic recovery and in 1934 he signed the Reciprocal Trade Agreements Act which gradually reduced tariffs between the United States and its trading partners.

3 Hoover encouraged voluntary agreements between workers and employers in an attempt to keep wages and production steady. However, such agreements failed to stop unemployment rising and wages falling.

Roosevelt used a more effective idea for his National Recovery Administration in 1933 (see page 24). He had codes drawn up setting out minimum wages and maximum hours, and employers came under strong pressure from the public to accept these codes (see source 2Q on page 25). In 1935 the Wagner Act (see page 31) also improved the workers' negotiating position, by forcing employers to recognise duly elected union representatives.

4 At Hoover's request, Congress voted $423 million for a government building programme to provide new jobs. One of the schemes paid for by this programme was the construction of the Hoover Dam on the Colorado River.

Roosevelt's Tennessee Valley Authority of 1933 (see page 21) and Works Progress Administration of 1935 (see page 29) also aimed to create work through building programmes, but their much larger budgets enabled them to provide a far greater number of jobs.

5 Hoover's administration set up the Reconstruction Finance Corporation in 1932. This provided loans totalling $1500 million to businesses, in order to enable them to increase employment. The introduction of tax cuts also helped businesses to take on more workers.

However, Hoover's programme made very little impact on the Depression. He had failed to understand the scale of the problems or to come up with new ideas that were capable of dealing with them. For example, his government left it to the American Red Cross to launch an emergency aid scheme. By 1932 the Red Cross had distributed 10 million barrels of flour to 5 million families, and had provided 66 million ready-made garments and 3 million blankets to the needy throughout the country.

The 1932 presidential election

Most American voters blamed the Republicans, who had governed the United States all through the 1920s, for the Depression. Hoover in particular could hardly expect his record as President to win him many votes.

Nevertheless, instead of offering new policies in the election campaign, Hoover concentrated on claiming that things would become far worse if the Democrats gained power. He warned that 'grass will grow in the streets of a hundred cities and a thousand towns, and weeds will over-run the fields' if Roosevelt won the presidency.

Gloomy speeches like this compared badly with the confidence that Roosevelt showed. The Democratic candidate's smile and optimism proved far more popular with the electorate than Hoover's grim looks.

This difference of presentation was important because in some ways the two candidates seemed to have similar policies; for example, government support for ailing businesses and job-creation schemes featured in the programmes of both candidates.

The main new ideas which Roosevelt introduced in the campaign were as follows:

● the identification of the lack of purchasing power of so many Americans as a major cause of the Depression. Hoover, on the other hand, believed that a drop in business confidence in the United States, and the general state of the world economy, were the major causes of the Depression;
● a promise to provide relief for the poor and the unemployed through bold and experimental measures whilst at the same time 'balancing the budget', that is, making sure that the government's spending did not exceed its income;
● more government control of the economy, to regulate production and protect workers against irresponsible employers;
● the repeal of the unpopular Prohibition Law which had made the production and sale of alcohol illegal since 1919. In the 1920s this law had been openly broken and gangsters had grown rich from organising illegal supplies of alcohol.

The election was held in November. Roosevelt obtained 57.4 per cent of the votes cast, to Hoover's 39.7 per cent. The remaining 2.9 per cent went to Socialist and Communist candidates. Roosevelt believed that the voters had given him a clear mandate (authority) to take vigorous action to deal with the Depression.

> When they told those who had no money
> 'Save your money'
> Those who had no money flashed back
> 'Would you ask those with nothing to eat
> to eat less?'
> **Source 1Y:** From section 36 of 'The People, Yes', by Carl Sandburg (1936).

11 Look at Source 1Y. From the evidence in this chapter, do you think the attitude towards poverty expressed in the last two lines of this source is more typical of Herbert Hoover or Franklin Roosevelt? Explain your answer.

12 If you had been an American voter in the presidential election of 1932, would you have voted for Hoover or for Roosevelt? Explain your choice.

The First New Deal

I pledge you, I pledge myself to a new deal for the American people.
(From Franklin Roosevelt's speech accepting his nomination as the Democratic candidate in the 1932 presidential election.)

The Brain Trust

In 1932 Franklin Roosevelt invited a group of university professors, lawyers, businessmen, experts from industry and social workers to help him to create this New Deal. They were able and confident, and between 1932 and 1936 they generated many new ideas, tried new methods to make these ideas succeed, and infected other people with their enthusiasm. These advisers were collectively known as the 'Brain Trust'.

Some commentators thought they were a bad influence on Roosevelt. For example H.L. Mencken, a journalist, described the members of the Brain Trust as 'professional uplifters and do-gooders . . . intolerable idiots'. However, Roosevelt relied heavily on their advice in his bid to beat the Depression. But what sort of people were they? Here are brief portraits of some of the main Brain Trust members.

At first *Raymond Moley* led the Brain Trust team and wrote some of Roosevelt's speeches. By 1936, however, his speeches for Roosevelt were being changed by other people and he withdrew from the Brain Trust. The leadership was then taken over by Benjamin Cohen and Thomas Corcoran. In the 1940 presidential election Moley supported Roosevelt's opponent, Wendell Wilkie, the Republican candidate.

Harry Hopkins remained a close adviser of Roosevelt throughout the New Deal and became director of several New Deal agencies. These included the Federal Emergency Relief Administration (FERA) (see page 18) and the Civil Works Administration (CWA) (see page 29) which were set up in 1933, and the Works Progress Administration (WPA) (see page 29) which was set up in 1935. The idea behind these agencies was Hopkins' belief that the Depression should be overcome by work relief (providing temporary jobs) rather than by simply giving money to the unemployed, which would serve to demoralise them. In 1938 Hopkins also became the Secretary of Commerce.

Before *Rexford Tugwell* joined the Brain Trust, he was a professor of Economics at Columbia University. He was an agricultural expert and became the deputy to Henry Wallace, the Secretary of Agriculture (see page 17). In 1935 Roosevelt also appointed him director of the Resettlement Administration (RA) (see page 35), which tried to help poor farmers.

Hugh Johnson, an ex-soldier was appointed head of the National Recovery Administration (NRA) (see page 24) by Roosevelt. He resigned in 1934 and turned against the New Deal because he thought it was too expensive.

Other leading advisers and assistants to the new President were Frances Perkins, Harold Ickes and Henry Wallace.

Frances Perkins was the first woman to become a member of the cabinet. She held the post of Secretary of Labour for twelve years, from 1933 to 1945. She was an expert in factory laws and industrial working conditions, but her main contribution to the New Deal was to persuade Roosevelt to support a national social security scheme (see page 28).

Harold Ickes was a lawyer who became Secretary of the Interior from 1933 to 1946. For a time he was also director of the Public Works Administration (PWA) (see page 26). However, he was criticised for taking too long to put his careful planning into operation and so delaying the recovery of the American economy.

Henry Wallace was Roosevelt's Secretary of Agriculture from 1933 to 1940 and Vice-President from 1940 to 1944. Wallace was an agricultural expert and had developed several improved strains of corn which were widely adopted. He also introduced the Agricultural Adjustment Act (see page 23).

The Hundred Days

In the spring of 1933, following his election as President of the United States, Roosevelt launched a crash programme of emergency measures to tackle the Depression. This programme was part of what became known as 'The Hundred Days', so-called because all the laws concerned were passed by Congress in exactly a hundred days, from 8 March to 16 June 1933.

The complete Hundred Days programme had three main aims:
RELIEF – to stop people starving and losing their property;
RECOVERY – to revive the American economy;
REFORM – to make the United States a better country to live in.

The main relief measures which made up the programme are outlined below.

1 Since 1930 5000 banks had run out of money and had been forced to close. One reason for this was that businesses to whom the banks had loaned money had gone bankrupt. Another was that savers who had deposited money with them became worried about its safety and asked for it back.

In March 1933 Roosevelt declared a four day 'bank holiday'. This meant that the government closed all the nation's banks to prevent people from withdrawing their savings. After carrying out detailed enquiries, the government allowed the banks that it decided were honest and well run to re-open; it also gave them government loans to continue operating, and insured their customers' deposits.

These reforms restored the public's confidence in the banking system. Customers who had earlier drawn out their money redeposited over $1 billion when the bank holiday ended. The finances of individuals and businesses were now more secure.

During the four days in which the banks were closed cash was very hard to obtain. In Source 2A the historian William Manchester describes some ingenious methods which people used to overcome this scarcity:

> A Wisconsin wrestler signed a contract to perform for a can of tomatoes and a peck of potatoes, an Ohio newspaper offered free advertisements in exchange for produce. A New York State senator arrived in Albany [the state capital] with twelve dozen eggs and a side of pork to see him through the week. In New York boxing fans bought tickets for the semi finals of the Golden Gloves tournament with clothes, jigsaw puzzles, spark plugs and copies of the Bible.
> Source 2A: From *The Glory and the Dream*, by William Manchester (1973).

2 The government devalued (reduced in value) the dollar by 40 per cent. It did this to make American products cheaper for foreigners to buy, in the hope of increasing export sales.

3 The government set up the Federal Emergency Relief Administration (FERA). FERA provided $500 million to help the individual states to pay for emergency schemes such as soup kitchens to feed the penniless.

Making sure that this FERA aid reached the people who needed it was not as easy as might be expected. In Source 2B the historian W.E. Leuchtenburg describes some of the drawbacks of the scheme:

> But the FERA program left much to be desired. People on direct relief felt humiliated. Applying for assistance was like making a formal admission of inadequacy. The applicant's esteem suffered another blow when an investigator entered his home to ascertain whether his application was truthful. Relief recipients were often too proud to go to the depot to accept surplus commodities lest they be recognised. One New York small businessman, determined to hold to the values he had learned, insisted on paying his rent regularly, even at the sacrifice of the family's food. The government, after learning how little the family spent for food, cut off the relief altogether, suspecting fraud.
> Source 2B: From *New Deal and War*, by W.E. Leuchtenburg (1964).

4 By 1933 a quarter of the United States' farmers had lost their land and thousands of householders had lost their homes. This was because they had not been able to pay their mortgages (loans made for the purchase of property).

Roosevelt persuaded Congress to pass laws to set up two new government bodies whose purpose was to help such property owners keep up their mortgage payments in future. The Farm Credit Administration (FCA) made loans to a fifth of all farmers, and Home Owners Loan Corporation (HOLC) made loans to over a million householders to prevent them losing their property. These measures also helped the banks by taking off them some of the pressure to provide loans for people in trouble.

5 Another important relief measure was the creation of the Civilian Conservation Corps (CCC). This was developed from a policy of setting the unemployed to work planting trees, which Roosevelt had introduced whilst he

was Governor of New York State. The CCC was also a way of improving land conservation, which was a major aim of the New Deal.

The CCC enlisted single men between the ages of 18 and 25 whose parents were unemployed. Living in camps run by the army and the Forest Service, they worked for up to six months on jobs such as planting trees, fighting forest fires, building reservoirs, clearing beaches and restoring historic battlefields. Almost 3 million men passed through the CCC scheme before the government brought it to an end in 1943.

The men who worked in the CCC camps were generally happy to do so. They were provided with food and clothing as well as wages of $30 a month, $25 of which they had to send home to their families. They also learned working skills which gave them a better chance of getting a job when they left the CCC.

Some people criticised the CCC as being a cheap labour scheme, but joining was not compulsory and there was never a shortage of volunteers. Sources 2C, 2D and 2E below give three different views about the CCC and its importance at the time:

> The CCC activity has probably been the most successful of anything we have done. There is not a word of complaint.
> **Source 2C:** President Roosevelt, speaking in 1934.

> Here they teach you how to pour concrete and lay stones and drive trucks, and if a boy wants to go and get a job after he's been in the Cs he'll know how to work.
> **Source 2D:** A 1934 CCC volunteer, speaking in 1938.

> They did more, of course, than reclaim and develop natural resources. They reclaimed and developed themselves. Their muscles hardened, their bodies filled out, their self-respect returned. They learned trades; more important they learned about America and they learned about other Americans.
> **Source 2E:** From *The Coming of the New Deal*, by the historian Arthur Schlesinger (1958).

Although unemployment was still high and industrial production low, at least the government was seen to be doing something about the Depression during the Hundred Days. This gave people confidence. Roosevelt encouraged this feeling with his 'fireside chats', informal radio broadcasts in which he explained his policies to the American people in simple, friendly language. He also encouraged people to write to him with their problems and received up to 8000 letters a day. This openness increased both Roosevelt's popularity and public support for the New Deal.

The sources below give an indication of how the American people reacted to Roosevelt's reforms:

> When people were able to survive the shock of having all the banks closed, and then see the banks open up, with their money protected, there began to be confidence. Good times were coming. Most of the legislation that came after didn't really help the public. The public helped itself, after it got confidence.
> **Source 2F:** From an interview given by Raymond Moley, a member of the Brain Trust, in the 1960s. In *Hard Times*, by Studs Terkel (1970).

> President Roosevelt has done his part; now you do something. Buy something – buy anything, paint your kitchen, send a telegram, give a party, get a car, pay a bill, rent a flat, fix your roof, get a haircut, see a show, build a house, take a trip, sing a song, get married.

> It does not matter what you do – but get going and keep going. This old world is starting to move.
> **Source 2G:** From a New Jersey factory notice board, 1933.

We had to go out and beg for coal, buy bread that's two, three days old. My dad died when I was an infant. I went to an orphan home till I was seventeen. I came out and my mother who was trying to raise my six older brothers and sisters couldn't afford another mouth to feed. So I joined. I was there for six months, planting trees and building forests in Michigan. Spent four and a half months fighting fires. I really enjoyed it. I had three wonderful square meals a day. No matter what they put on the table we ate and were glad to get it. They sure made a man out of you because you learned that everybody was equal.

Source 2H: From an interview about the CCC given by Blackie Gold, a car dealer. In *Hard Times*, by Studs Terkel (1970).

Source 2I: A CCC camp headquarters.

1 a) Explain what the Brain Trust's job was.

b) Name two members of the Brain Trust.

c) Describe the part played in the Hundred Days by one of them.

2 Describe two different ways in which President Roosevelt tried to give Americans confidence that the Depression could be overcome.

3 Look at Source 2G. Select three of the suggestions made in this source which you think would have helped Roosevelt's aim of economic recovery. Explain how the actions you have selected would have done this.

4 Look at sources 2H and 2I.

a) What evidence is there in Source 2H that the speaker is talking about the Civilian Conservation Corps?

b) The CCC was supervised by the Army and the Forest Service. What evidence is there in Source 2H that the CCC was organised on army lines?

c) Using Sources 2H and 2I and the information about the CCC on pages 18–19, explain what you think would appeal most about camp life to those who joined.

5 Look at Sources 2F and 2H.

a) In what way does Source 2H contradict the claim made in Source 2F that government legislation did not help people?

b) What does this suggest to you about the way that a historian should use evidence?

The Tennessee Valley Authority (TVA)

The government 'alphabet agencies' about which you have just read provided immediate relief and had mainly short-term aims. The Hundred Days programme also set up other alphabet agencies which had the longer-term aims of recovery and reform. The Tennessee Valley Authority (TVA) was the first of these.

The Tennessee river and its tributaries drain an area that is as large as England and Scotland combined. The 4.5 million people who lived there in the early 1930s had been badly affected by the Depression. The TVA helped them by improving five existing dams and building 20 new ones. The first of these was Norris Dam, which is shown in Source 2J, whilst still under construction.

Source 2J: The Norris Dam.

Dams like this did more than just provide jobs for their builders. They also stopped floods and soil erosion, both of which had been serious problems in this area of high rainfall. Flood control made possible cheap river transport over 1043 kilometres of waterways and benefited agriculture and industry in the region.

The power stations built at the dams made the TVA the biggest producer of electricity in the United States. This power was sold at a third of its former price, a change welcomed not only by domestic consumers, but by farmers and industries such as light engineering, which moved into the area and helped its economic recovery.

Farmers received other benefits from the TVA. The Authority manufactured and sold low-cost fertilisers and taught farmers how to use them to restore fertility to their soil. It also encouraged farmers to prevent soil erosion by contour ploughing and planting trees.

These developments benefited six other states besides Tennessee, as the map in Source 2K shows.

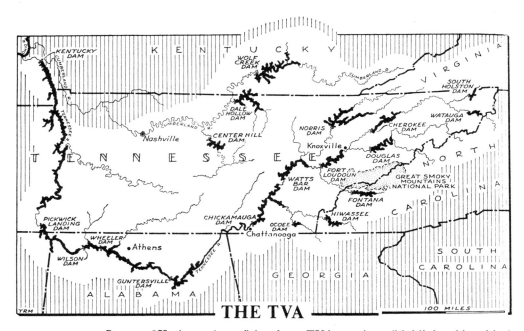

Source 2K: Areas benefiting from TVA services (highlighted in white).

However, the availability of cheap electricity was not welcomed by everyone. Some private companies which supplied power went out of business because they could not compete with TVA prices. Sources 2L and 2M give two opposing views of the TVA:

> The American people are paying more than half a billion dollars for eleven dams, chiefly designed to supply power to one area [the Tennessee Valley]. But this power is to be supplied to this area at less than cost. In other words the TVA will operate annually at a deficit, and these annual deficits must, of course, be paid out of the pockets of the taxpayers.
> **Source 2L:** Wendell Wilkie, the head of a private company which also supplied electricity, speaking in 1940. He sold the company to the TVA in 1939.

> This river [the Tennessee] had many potential assets. It could yield hydro-electric power for the comfort of the people in their homes, could promote prosperity on their farms and foster the development of industry. But the same river, by the very same dams, could be made to provide fun for fishermen and fish for food, pleasure from boating and swimming, a water supply for home and factories.
> **Source 2M:** David Lilienthal, the head of the TVA, writing in his book, *Democracy on the March* (1944).

6 The description of the TVA on pages 21–22 mentions several benefits provided to local people by the TVA.

a) What were these benefits?

b) What additional benefits could the Tennessee river provide according to Source 2M?

c) Use the information in your answers to a) and b) to help you to design and draw a publicity poster for the TVA.

7 Read Sources 2L and 2M.

a) Why might you expect the writer in Source 2L to be critical of the TVA, and the one in Source 2M to be full of praise for it?

b) What does this suggest that you need to know about the *origins* of historical information or opinions, before deciding how valuable they are?

c) Which writer's point of view would you have agreed with if you had lived in the Tennessee valley in the 1930s? Explain your choice.

The Agricultural Adjustment Act (AAA)

Congress passed this Hundred Days Act in an attempt to increase the incomes of farmers, who in 1933 still made up 30 per cent of the population of the United States. This was to be done by the government paying farmers to destroy existing crops and to cut back on future production. Roosevelt hoped that this plan would increase the prices farmers could obtain for their produce and therefore give them extra cash to buy manufactured goods.

Many farmers increased their incomes with the help of AAA subsidies (payments). But as the cost of manufactured goods was also rising, their standard of living did not improve at first. In fact, some southern tenant farmers (farmers who did not own land but rented it) became worse off after the AAA was passed. This was because the owners of the land evicted them in order to qualify for subsidies by reducing their cotton acreage.

However, as prices stabilised, farmers who owned their land benefited from the AAA, although the reluctance of some farmers to join the scheme remained a serious obstacle to its success. Destroying produce was unnatural for farmers, and many could not be persuaded to take part.

Two contemporary views of the effect of the Depression on farmers are given in Sources 2N and 2O:

> I talked to one man in a restaurant in Chicago. He told me of his experience in raising sheep. He said that he had killed 3000 sheep this fall [autumn] and thrown them down the canyon, because it cost $1.10 to ship a sheep and then he would get less than a dollar for it . . . the farmers are being pauperized by the poverty of industrial populations, and the industrial populations are being pauperized by the poverty of the farmers. Neither has the money to buy the product of the other; hence we have overproduction and underconsumption at the same time and in the same country.
> **Source 2N:** Part of the evidence given by a reporter to an investigation into unemployment made by the US Congress in 1932.

> Hog [pig] prices have gone to hell. What were they – four, five cents a pound? The farmers are starving to death. We decided to slaughter pregnant pigs. That lowered the supply going to market and the prices immediately went up. Then a great cry went up from the press about Henry Wallace, the Secretary for Agriculture, slaughtering these little pigs. You'd think they were precious babies.

You had a similar situation in cotton. Prices were down to four cents a pound and the cost of producing was probably ten. So a program was initiated to plough up cotton. A third of the crop if I remember. Cotton prices went up to ten cents, maybe eleven.

Source 2O: From an interview given by C.B. Baldwin, Assistant to the Secretary of Agriculture. In *Hard Times*, by Studs Terkel (1970).

---

8 a) Explain how the AAA was supposed to benefit farmers.

b) Which group of farmers did *not* benefit from the AAA? Explain why.

9 a) Look at Source 2N. Why had a farmer thrown 3000 of his sheep into a canyon instead of selling them?

b) Look at Source 2O:

(i) What effect did killing animals have on farmers' incomes?

(ii) Why did it have this effect?

(iii) By how much did cotton prices increase after the introduction of the plan to plough up a third of the cotton crop? Why did they increase?

10 a) Why do you think the press criticised Henry Wallace (Source 2O) for ordering the killing of pigs?

b) Can you suggest any alternative solutions to the problem of 'overproduction and underconsumption' (Source 2N)?

The National Recovery Administration (NRA)

The main problems faced by business and industry during the Depression were low prices and insufficient demand. This sort of economic situation is referred to as a deflationary spiral. It is caused by having more goods for sale than people can afford to buy.

To overcome this problem, Roosevelt introduced the National Recovery Administration (NRA) as another part of his Hundred Days programme. He described his plan as 'the most important and far reaching legislation ever enacted by the American Congress'.

The intention of the NRA was to persuade industries to introduce codes of fair practice which would maintain wages and prices above a certain level and, in some cases, restrict production. Employers were encouraged to improve working conditions by providing a minimum weekly wage and a maximum working day, by abolishing child labour and by accepting the right of their workers to organise labor, or trade, unions. In return, businesses which co-operated with the scheme had the right to display the blue eagle symbol (see Source 2R on page 25) and consumers were encouraged to buy only from them.

Roosevelt tried to build up enthusiasm for the NRA by organising a huge advertising campaign, which included the New York parade described in Source 2Q below. At first the campaign seemed to be working. Industrial production, prices and wages all rose.

However the NRA faced great difficulties. Some employers broke the codes of employment which they had agreed with their workers. Although in theory they could be prosecuted for this, many were not. Another problem was that small businesses often found it difficult to keep to the terms of the codes and still make enough profit to continue operating.

Impressions of the NRA, and how it affected people, can be gained from the primary sources below.

> In war, in the gloom of a night attack, soldiers wear a bright badge on their shoulders to be sure that comrades do not fire on comrades. On that principle those who co-operate in this programme must know each other at a glance. That is why we have provided a badge of honour for this purpose, a simple design with the legend 'We do our part', and I ask that all those who join with me shall display that badge prominently.
> **Source 2P:** Franklin D. Roosevelt, explaining his NRA badge plan in 1933.

> ### 1,500,000 CHEER VAST NRA PARADE; MARCH OF 250,000 CITY'S GREATEST; DEMONSTRATION LASTS TILL MIDNIGHT
> Under the golden glow of Fifth Avenue's festive arc lights the legions of the Blue Eagle marched until midnight last night before hundreds of thousands of spectators whom weariness could not drive away from a demonstration of confidence and enthusiasm such as had not been seen for half a generation.
>
> More than a quarter of a million strong – employers and employees side by side – the President's NRA Day parade took the evening as well as the afternoon in which to manifest its faith in President Roosevelt's recovery program.
>
> Governor Lehman, Mayor O'Brien and other officials were still in the stand in front of the main building of the New York Public Library at Forty-first Street when the last detachment – fifteen makers of artificial flowers – marched by at 11.22 pm.
>
> It was the greatest march in New York City's history, the reviewing officials agreed. That note of superlative was echoed along the dim-lit canyon of Fifth Avenue throughout the evening by the man in the street and his wife too, and the children for whom the day was an important page in a new chapter of history.
> **Source 2Q:** From *the New York Times*, 14 September 1933.

Source 2R: A cartoon from the *New York World-Telegram*, 18 September 1933.

> When you all work for NRA
> You work shorter hours and get the same pay.
> **Source 2S:** From an Appalachian folk song of the 1930s.

> We used to work eight hours and feel fine when the quitting whistle blew. Now we work six hours and are dead-tired.
> **Source 2T:** Part of a rubber worker's letter to an Akron newspaper, 1935.

I think the NRA is a great thing. It has put more money in my pay and the short hours has made a new person out of me, as when I used to work 11 hours I could not feel like going anywhere to have a good time. Now I have plenty of time for rest before play. I hope there will always be an NRA.

Source 2U: The opinion of a North Carolina cotton mill worker, given to John Spivak, a reporter, in 1934.

'How're things?' I asked. She was too busy to stop and I walked alongside.
'All right,' she said, swiftly. Her eyes followed the turning spindles.
'Better since the NRA?'
'Yeah.'
'How much do you make?'
'Twelve-fifty.'
'How many hours?'
'Eight. We used to work twelve.'
'Less hours and more pay, eh? NRA do that?'
'Yeah. But we got doubled-up.'
'What's that?'
'Doubled-up. Stretched-out. We got to do twice as much work as we used to. Got to work faster, too. So it's all the same as before. We get exactly what we got before.'
'How much was that?'
'Six dollars a week. Now we work twice as much so we get twelve dollars. No difference.'
'But you have four hours extra a day, haven't you?'
'Yeah. But what good's that? I'm too tired to go out when I get through.'

Source 2V: The opinion of a North Carolina cotton mill worker given to John Spivak, a reporter, in 1934.

Source 2W: A 1933 newspaper cartoon from the *Philadelphia Record*.

The NRA was set up under a law called the National Recovery Act. This law also established another important organisation called the Public Works Administration (PWA). The PWA was administered by Harold Ickes, the Secretary of the Interior, and its aim was to increase employment and business activity through the construction of roads and public buildings.

The PWA spent $4250 million on a total of 34,000 projects between 1934 and 1939. Roosevelt hoped that this would increase consumer spending power and enable people to afford the higher prices which the NRA would create.

---

11 a) What main problems did the NRA try to overcome?

b) Describe how it tackled any *two* of them.

c) Look at Source 2P. Quote two phrases which prove that membership of the NRA was not compulsory.

12 Look at Sources 2Q and 2R.

a) The parade and the cartoon had the same aim. What do you think it was?

b) What object is the eagle holding in its right claw? Explain the significance of both this object and of the zig-zag lines shooting from the eagle's right claw.

c) Who was 'Secretary Perkins'?

13 Read Sources 2S, 2T, 2U and 2V.

a) Write down the letters of the sources which indicate that:

(i) workers benefited from the NRA;
(ii) the NRA had disadvantages for workers.

b) According to the sources you have mentioned in a) (ii), why were some workers worse off under the NRA?

c) How would you account for the differences of opinion about the NRA expressed in these four sources?

14 Look at Source 2W.

a) Identify the man in the cartoon. Provide proof, from the cartoon, for your answer.

b) How is the Depression depicted in the cartoon?

c) What means of fighting the Depression does the cartoonist show the man using?

d) By referring to one feature of the cartoon, explain the meaning of the caption 'His greatest fight lies ahead'.

The Second New Deal

To work hard, to live hard, to die hard, and then to go to hell after all would be too damned hard.
(From section 30 of 'The People, Yes' published by the poet Carl Sandburg in 1936.)

Beginning in 1935, President Roosevelt began to introduce more important New Deal measures. One of these provided a form of relief which was new to the United States – social welfare.

The Social Security Act 1935

In 1933 Roosevelt appointed Frances Perkins (see also page 17) as his Secretary of Labour. She was the first woman to become a member of the cabinet and she helped to convince Roosevelt that the United States needed an insurance programme for those who were handicapped because of unemployment, old age or illness.

The Social Security Act of 1935 was the first attempt to provide for the welfare of society's weaker members on a national scale. It introduced old age pensions for people over 65. Beginning in 1940, they were to receive between $10 and $85 a month, paid for from taxes on earnings and on employers' profits. The Act also introduced unemployment insurance and aid for the blind and physically handicapped, and for mothers with dependent children, who were paid up to $20 a month.

It was intended that unemployment insurance would be provided by individual states and localities, with aid from the Federal government in the form of payroll tax rebates. However, so many people applied for unemployment pay that many areas tried to avoid having to pay it, as the road sign at the Idaho state boundary in Source 3A shows.

Source 3A: Department of Public Assistance sign, Idaho.

The aid provided to the blind, handicapped and dependent mothers and children was known as 'categorical assistance'. It was based on the 'matching grant' principle, that is, the Federal government contributed as much money for this group as did each state. Obviously, this meant that better off states had far more money to distribute than others. For example, in 1939 dependent mothers and children in Arkansas received $8.10 a month, whilst in Massachusetts the rate was $61.07 a month.

Ex-President Hoover and other conservatives disapproved of social security. They thought that it encouraged people to be lazy and that it took away their dignity by treating them as numbers rather than as individuals.

Many liberals were also unhappy with the Social Security Act. They did not consider the pension to be sufficient for old people to live on, and felt that delaying the start of payments until 1940 was unnecessary. They also criticised the Act because, apart from categorical assistance, it made no provision for a health insurance scheme.

However, President Roosevelt considered social security to be one of the most important parts of the New Deal. He summed up his attitude to it in his annual message to Congress in 1938.

> Government has the final responsibility for the well-being of its citizens. If private endeavour fails to provide work for willing hands and relief for the unfortunate, those suffering hardship from no fault of their own have a right to call upon the government for aid; and a government worthy of its name must make fitting response.
>
> **Source 3B:** From Roosevelt's annual message to Congress, 1938.

Source 3C: A cartoonist's comment on the Social Security Act.

The Works Progress Administration (WPA) 1935

The creation of jobs was a top priority in Roosevelt's plan to overcome the Depression. In 1933 the President had established the Civil Works Administration (CWA) to provide people without jobs with temporary work. C.B. Baldwin, a government official at the time, remembered the CWA like this:

> They set up this CWA very hurriedly. Any guy could just walk into the county office – they were set up all over the country – and get a job. Leaf raking, cleaning up libraries, painting the town hall . . . Within a period of sixty days four million people were put to work.
>
> **Source 3D:** From an interview given by C.B. Baldwin. In *Hard Times*, by Studs Terkel (1970).

The extra purchasing power the CWA created contributed to the recovery of the American economy. But some businessmen felt that the jobs it created were pointless and a waste of money, and refused to support them. This caused Roosevelt to end the CWA in 1934.

Although by 1935 unemployment in the United States had fallen by 3 million since 1933, 10 million people were still without work. So, in 1935 Roosevelt appointed Harry Hopkins (see page 16), the director of the CWA, as director of a new agency, the Works Progress Administration (WPA).

By 1941 the WPA had provided work for a further 3 million Americans. Most of the new jobs it provided were connected with building schemes. For example, the WPA was responsible for 800,000 kilometres of roads being laid, and the construction of 2500 hospitals, 600 airports and 100,000 bridges.

The WPA also made an important contribution to dealing with the problem of the Dust Bowl (see pages 8–9). Its workers helped the Forest Service to erect a windbreak across the Great Plains by planting trees along a line stretching from North Dakota to Oklahoma. The windbreak was 160 kilometres wide and 1600 kilometres long and required millions of trees to be planted. Governor Murray of Oklahoma, among others, believed the idea was impractical – 'like trying to grow hair on a bald head'. Nevertheless, it stopped further soil erosion and helped the Great Plains to become fertile again.

Some 7 per cent of the WPA's budget of $11 billion was used for arts projects. The government employed writers, actors, painters and musicians for jobs such as painting murals to decorate inner city areas, and creating sculptures to celebrate the achievements of the New Deal. Some artists were paid to do their own work. One of these was Gutzon Borglum, who sculpted the giant heads of Presidents Washington, Jefferson, Lincoln and Theodore Roosevelt out of a mountainside in South Dakota (see Source 3E).

Source 3E: Gutzon Borglum's sculptures of American presidents, Mount Rushmore, South Dakota.

The WPA also supervised the National Youth Administration (NYA). This provided part-time jobs for over 2 million students and 2.6 million other youngsters who had left school, but were not involved in other relief schemes such as the CCC.

The WPA did more to reduce unemployment than any other alphabet agency. Nevertheless, it was still criticised for paying people to do jobs that were not worthwhile. For example, the writer John Steinbeck was employed by the WPA to count all the dogs in the Monterey Peninsula in California.

1 With which New Deal measures do you associate a) Frances Perkins, and b) Harry Hopkins?

2 a) Which group in American society do you think benefited the most from the Social Security Act? Explain your choice.

b) Look at Source 3C. Is the artist criticising or approving of the Social Security Act? Explain your answer.

3 a) How many people obtained work through the WPA between 1935 and 1941?

b) List three types of new job created by the WPA.

c) (i) Why did Governor Murray criticise the work of the WPA in Oklahoma?

(ii) For what other reasons was the WPA criticised?

(iii) If you had been Harry Hopkins, how might you have replied to these criticisms?

Labor laws, unions and strikes

At the start of the Depression American labor unions, were weak. Section 7a of the National Recovery Act stated that 'employees shall have the right to organize and bargain collectively through representatives of their own choosing, and shall be free from the interference, restraint or coercion of employers.' Many employees ignored this provision, however, and a wave of strikes in 1934 and 1935 encouraged Congress to pass a measure introduced by Senator Robert Wagner, which was intended to give the unions greater protection.

The Wagner Act of 1935 set up a National Labour Relations Board which arranged for elections to be held so that workers for particular firms could vote on whether they wanted to be represented by a union. The Board could also prevent employers from sacking workers for being union members, and oblige them to listen to workers' demands for improved working conditions.

This government support encouraged more workers to join unions like the United Rubber Workers and the United Automobile Workers. Such unions joined together to form the Congress of Industrial Organisations (CIO) (see page 33), which increased its membership to over 6 million by 1945.

Nevertheless, despite New Deal efforts like the NRA (see page 24) and the Wagner Act to encourage co-operation between workers and employers, the 1930s was a time of stress between them. The events described below are some examples of that stress.

Shape ups

In 1934 San Francisco longshoremen (dockers) went on strike to try to force their employers to end the 'shape up' system. This required longshoremen to assemble at the docks each day in the hope of being selected for work that day or shift by the company foremen. The effects of the shape-up system were insecurity and corruption; workers could not count on regular employment and some even bribed foremen to hire them.

The San Francisco employers brought in strikebreakers to keep the docks open. However, the dockers were supported by the Teamsters' Union, whose lorry drivers refused to transport goods which had been unloaded by strikebreakers. The San Francisco police clashed with pickets who were preventing strikebreakers getting into the docks to work. The *New York Times* newspaper described an incident which occurred on 4 July 1934:

Mounted and foot police swung their clubs and hurled tear-gas bombs, strikers hurled bricks and rocks, battered heads with clubs and railroad spikes and smashed windows. The police relentlessly drove the pickets behind the freightcar barriers.

Twenty-five police and pickets were casualties of this battle.
Source 3F: *New York Times*, 5 July 1934.

The violence in San Francisco prompted the Governor of California to reinforce the police with members of the National Guard (state troops), and in a further clash two pickets were killed. This prompted a general strike in several west coast cities.

President Roosevelt felt that the employers had provoked the trouble, but the NRA director, General Hugh Johnson, supported the employers. After four days the unions, feeling betrayed, called off the strike. The shape-up system continued as before.

Stretch-outs

The largest of the New Deal strikes was a result of 'stretch-outs' in the textile industry. The stretch-out was a method used by employers to cut costs. They would extend the workers' hours or increase the number of looms a worker had to operate whilst paying the same wages.

After the NRA was set up, membership of the United Textile Workers Union rose from 27,500 in 1932 to 270,000 in 1934. The NRA issued a code of employment for the textile industry which set a minimum wage of $13 a week for textile workers. Many employers ignored the code, however, and the stretch-outs continued.

The textile strike began in September 1935 in North Carolina and spread rapidly through the textile manufacturing areas of the east coast states. At first the union sent 'flying squads' of pickets to persuade textile workers in isolated communities to join the strike. But when the pickets became involved in clashes with employers and non-strikers, union leaders stopped using them.

Nevertheless the violence continued. The *New York Times* described what happened at Honea Path, South Carolina, on 6 September 1934:

Without warning came the first shots, followed by many others, and for a few minutes there was bedlam. Striker after striker fell to the ground, with the cries of wounded men sounding over the field and men and women, running shrieking from the scene.
Source 3G: *New York Times*, 7 September 1934.

Seven strikers were killed and 20 wounded in this incident. The effect was to extend the strike and increase the number and size of the clashes. In Georgia, Governor Talmadge declared martial law (that is, the maintenance of law and order was delegated to the military authorities), strike leaders were imprisoned without charges and the National Guard killed 13 strikers.

On 22 September, however, the Union ended the strike, having been promised an investigation into conditions in the textile industry. President Roosevelt encouraged employers to re-hire workers who had been on strike, but the Union claimed that 339 mill owners refused to do so, and that thousands lost their jobs.

So in 1934, despite the existence of the NRA, workers were often not supported by the government in disputes with employers, who often used force and threats to defeat strikers. The year ended with no noticeable gains in the struggle for union recognition, nor in the improvement of working conditions.

Sitdowns

Strikes were also caused when employers tried to find a way round the NRA minimum wage and maximum hours regulations by forcing their employees to work faster. This happened to workers in the rubber industry in Akron, Ohio, in 1935. They responded with a new strike tactic – the 'sitdown'.

> At first the sitdowns were effective, short and peaceful: Sitting by their machines, cauldrons, boilers and work benches they talked. Some realized *for the first time how important they were in the process of rubber production.* Twelve men had practically stopped the works! Almost any dozen or score of them could do it! In some departments six could do it! . . . This sudden suspension of production was costing the company many hundreds of dollars every minute . . . In less than an hour the dispute was settled – full victory for the men!
>
> **Source 3H:** L. Adamic, a New York journalist writing in 1935. He visited Akron and interviewed striking rubber workers.

However, workers continued to be made to work faster, especially in the automobile, or car, industry. In 1934 the NRA Division of Research and Planning declared that such speed-ups were the most unpopular of all working practices. The unions hit back by organising sitdowns in all General Motors' factories in 1937.

The effect was dramatic: only 60,000 vehicles were completed in January 1937, out of a production target of 224,000. In the first ten days of February General Motors made only 151 cars throughout the entire country. Violent clashes between police and strikers occurred, but the sitdowns continued and in April 1937 General Motors gave in:

> The inhuman high speed is *no more.* We now have a voice, and have slowed up the speed of the line. And we are now treated as human beings, and not as part of the machinery. The high pressure is taken off . . . It proves clearly that united we stand, divided we fall.
>
> **Source 3I:** Alfred Lockhart, a General Motors worker who had opposed the strike, writing to a friend in 1937.

The sitdown tactic spread to other industries and was very successful. Together with the protection provided by the Wagner Act (see page 31), it was responsible later that year for forcing US Steel – which had the reputation of being the most anti-union of employers – to negotiate a fair practice code without a strike.

The Memorial Day Massacre

An important result of the strikes of the New Deal period was the formation in 1935 of a new grouping of unions, the Congress of Industrial Organisations (CIO). Until then, individual unions had been linked to the American Federation of Labor (AFL), which protected the interests of skilled workers in various crafts. Unskilled or semi-skilled workers in basic industries such as rubber, steel and car manufacture had no central organisation to help them.

The leader of the CIO was John L. Lewis, the spokesman of the mine workers. Lewis believed that negotiating contracts between employers and workers was the best way for industry to prosper. These contracts could benefit both workers and employers by making strikes unnecessary.

Despite these aims, the formation of the CIO did not end the violence between workers and employers during the Depression. In 1937 the Republic Steel Company in Chicago refused to negotiate a contract, so the CIO organised a strike of its workers. On Memorial Day (31 May), a public holiday, strikers and their families marching outside the factory were attacked by 500 policemen armed with tear gas and pistols. Ten marchers were killed and 100 were wounded, some with bullets in their backs. An investigation organised by Senator Robert La Follette Jr reported that:

> . . . provocation for the police assault did not go beyond abusing language and the throwing of isolated missiles from the rear ranks of the marchers .

. . From all the evidence we think it plain that the force employed by the police was far in excess of that which the occasion required. Its use must be ascribed either to gross inefficiency in the performance of the police duty, or a deliberate attempt to intimidate the strikers.

Source 3J: From the Report on the 1937 Memorial Day Massacre, by Senator Robert La Follette Jr.

Senator La Follette's report was based on eyewitness evidence and film of the event taken by Paramount for a newsreel. Source 3K gives three extracts from the evidence given by Dr Lewis Andreas, who had been asked by CIO pickets to set up a First Aid station outside the Republic Steel plant on Memorial Day:

What happened was this: There were a few rocks thrown at the police when the shooting started. Or even before. They all turned and ran. As they were running the police shot into them. The police weren't all bad. Some of them quit the force because of the incident. They couldn't stand what happened . . .

The misrepresentation in the newspapers was so great. There was a picture in the back page of the 'Tribune' for instance: a little old guy lying on the prairie in his white shirt, blood streaming down his face and Lieutenant Kilroy beating the hell out of him with his club. The caption said: 'Striker Beats Up Police at Republic Steel Riot.' A few of us said this will be called a historical fact some day unless we do something about it . . .

All of a sudden I heard some popping going on and a blue haze rising. I said 'My God, tear gas. What do you do for that?' I couldn't remember what the medical books said. About three minutes later, they started bringing the wounded, shot. There were about fifty shot. Ten of them died. One little boy was shot in the heel. I took care of him. One woman was shot in the arm. They were lying there, bleeding, bullet wounds in the belly, in the leg and all over. All sorts of fractures, lacerations . . . I had absolutely no preparation at all for this.

Source 3K: Extracts from evidence given by Dr Lewis Andreas to the investigation of the 1937 Memorial Day Massacre.

Source 3L: The Memorial Day Massacre outside the Republic Steel Company plant in Chicago, 31 May 1937.

4 a) List five industries which experienced strikes in the period 1934–7.

b) How did employers try to end the strikes mentioned in this section?

c) Choose any *two* of these strikes and explain why you think the strikes you have chosen were, or were not, justified.

5 Read the section on the Memorial Day Massacre and study Source 3L.

a) Are (i) Senator La Follette's report (Source 3J), (ii) Dr Andreas' evidence (Source 3K) and (iii) the photograph (Source 3L), primary or secondary historical sources? Explain your answers.

b) What evidence is there in Source 3K that:

(i) the strikers were responsible for the Massacre;
(ii) the police were responsible for the Massacre;
(iii) the strikers were attacked with other weapons, besides guns?

c) The official report of the Massacre gave 100 as the number wounded, but Dr Andreas estimated that only 50 people were wounded. How do you explain this contradiction?

d) Which side do you think the Chicago newspaper the *Tribune* supported in the Republic Steel strike? Extract words or phrases from Dr Andreas' evidence to support your choice.

e) Does Source 3L support or contradict Dr Andreas' evidence? Explain your answer.

f) In what ways can (i) eye-witness accounts and (ii) photographs of events be both helpful and misleading as pieces of historical evidence?

The Resettlement Administration (RA) 1935 and the Farm Security Administration (FSA) 1937

The New Deal neglected many Americans – sharecroppers, tenant farmers, farm labourers and migrating workers, unskilled workers and the unemployed Negroes. They were left outside the new order.
Source 3M: From *Towards a New Past*, by B.J. Bernstein (1969).

The Agricultural Adjustment Act of 1933 (see page 23) had only helped farm owners. Sharecroppers who farmed the owner's land for a share of the crop, tenants who rented their land, and farm workers who neither owned nor rented land received no help from it. In fact, by encouraging farmers to plant less the AAA forced many sharecroppers, especially cotton sharecroppers in southern states, and tenants to leave the land. Landlords had no reason to keep on sharecroppers when there were no crops to be harvested, so they evicted them. Source 3N shows evicted sharecroppers in Parkin, Arkansas, in January 1936.

In 1935 President Roosevelt set up the Resettlement Administration (RA) to provide sharecroppers, tenants and farm workers with help. Rexford Tugwell, a 'Brain Trust' member (see page 16), was appointed director of the RA. It aimed to move 500,000 families to better land and resettle them in newly built houses in new rural communities.

An earlier scheme had given low-paid farm labourers plots on the outskirts of large cities so that they could supplement their incomes by growing crops. However, the scheme did not have sufficient funds to fulfil its aims. Only 4441 families were resettled and plots were provided only in Washington, Cincinnatti and Milwaukee.

Source 3N: Evicted sharecroppers, Parkin, Arkansas, January 1936.

Source 3O gives an impression of the conditions endured by sharecropper families:

> They live in steady shame and insult of discomforts, insecurities and inferiorities, piecing these together into whatever semblance of comfortable living they can, and the whole of it is a stark nakedness of makeshifts and the lack of means.
>
> **Source 3O:** From *Let Us Now Praise Famous Men*, an account of the effects of the Depression on sharecroppers in words and pictures. Compiled in the 1930s by James Agee and Walker Evans, for the Farm Security Administration.

In 1937 Roosevelt replaced the RA with the Farm Security Administration (FSA). This was more successful in helping poor farmers than the earlier schemes. By 1944 the FSA had helped to resettle 11,000 families and provide 41,000 long-term low-interest loans to help tenants and sharecroppers to buy their own farms. The FSA also established labour camps, which helped migrants from the Dust Bowl looking for work in California to improve their living conditions. Typically, however, the improvement was only slight, as Sources 3P and 3Q indicate.

Source 3P: Cardboard shacks, the winter homes of migrant farm workers in Imperial Valley, California.

Source 3Q: Migrant's family and home in an FSA labour camp in California.

The FSA might have done more, but it was opposed by members of Congress from the southern states. One reason for their opposition was that the FSA provided integrated camps and medical schemes for both black and white migrant workers at a time when the races were still strictly segregated in the South.

Pictures of rural poverty

The photographs in this section were taken by Walker Evans and Dorothea Lange, who also worked for the FSA Photography Unit.

Source 3R: 'Woman of the High Plains', by Dorothea Lange.

Source 3S: 'Sharecropper's Kitchen Wall', by Walker Evans.

Source 3T: 'Sharecropper Family', by Walker Evans.

6 a) Look at Source 3R and read the section on the Resettlement Administration. Suggest a possible reason for the apparent distress of the woman in the picture.

b) Look at Sources 3S and 3T. What evidence is there in these pictures that sharecroppers were poor in the 1930s?

c) 'Photographs can sometimes tell lies.' Do you agree or disagree with this statement? Explain your answer.

7 Using Sources 3R, 3S and 3T together with the written extracts in Sources 3M and 3O:

a) write a letter to the FSA from a sharecropper describing your problems and criticising the FSA for not helping you more;

b) write a reply from an FSA official which tries to answer the criticisms and describes the achievements of the FSA.

The Last Phase of the New Deal

Franklin 'Depression' Roosevelt.
Franklin 'Double-Crossing' Roosevelt.
(Two nicknames used for Franklin Delano Roosevelt in 1936.)

The approach of the 1936 presidential election

In November 1936 a presidential election took place in the United States. This provided the voters with their first chance to pass judgement on Franklin Roosevelt and the New Deal.

The President had many critics. Their main concerns were the financial cost of the New Deal, the continuing high rate of unemployment, the failure of relief measures to help those for whom they were intended, and the methods Roosevelt used.

There was some truth in what Roosevelt's critics said. The New Deal schemes were expensive and taxes had had to be increased in order to pay for them. These taxes were mainly on inheritance and income and they were 'graduated' so that the rich paid more than the poor. Those people who were receiving assistance under New Deal relief schemes paid no taxes at all.

Some critics were especially worried about the cost of the New Deal because certain aspects of its policies seemed so wasteful. For example, some people found it difficult to approve of the Agricultural Adjustment Act (see page 23) because of the destruction of crops and livestock which it required. The Works Progress Administration (see page 29) was criticised for paying people to do unnecessary jobs or merely to 'lean on shovels' all day.

Despite the New Deal and its alphabet agencies the United States still had 9 million unemployed in 1936. Although this was a reduction of over 3 million since Roosevelt became President in 1932, it was seen as failure by his critics. Equally serious was the fact that some groups who had been badly affected by the Depression had still received no help by 1936. For example, the old did not receive pensions (see page 28) until 1940 and the plight of many sharecroppers remained desperate, despite the work of the Resettlement Administration.

However, the most common criticism of the New Deal was not that it did not go far enough; it was that it went too far. The United States had no tradition of the government providing social security, for example, and some people thought that the Social Security Act (see page 28) was somehow un-American. Both the Tennessee Valley Authority (see page 21) and the National Recovery Administration (see page 24) were criticised for creating competition in business and economic life between the government and its citizens. The economic planning involved in the Agricultural Adjustment Act (see page 23) reminded Roosevelt's critics of fascism in Hitler's Germany or of communism in Stalin's Soviet Union. He was accused of acting like a dictator and of making the government too powerful.

Roosevelt welcomed bitter criticism of this sort. It enabled him to characterise his opponents as 'the lunatic fringe'.

Some of Roosevelt's critics

In the period leading up to the 1936 election the following people were particularly critical of Roosevelt and the New Deal.

Huey Long was Governor of the state of Louisiana. In 1934 he proposed the 'Share Our Wealth' scheme as an alternative to Roosevelt's New Deal. The scheme proposed to take money from the rich and give it to the poor so that every family would have an income of $2500 a year, and a home worth $5000. Long intended to challenge Roosevelt for the presidency in the 1936 election, but he was assassinated in September 1935. The 'Share Our Wealth' movement survived, however, under the leadership of Gerald Smith.

Dr Francis Townsend claimed to have a better plan to deal with the Depression than Roosevelt. It was very simple: everyone over the age of 60 was to be given a pension of $200 a month, which would be paid for by a 2 per cent sales tax. Townsend believed that when people spent these pensions on goods and services the economy would revive and material prosperity be restored. He also claimed that his plan would create jobs for the young by forcing workers over the age of 60 to retire. As the 1930 census had listed 4 million people in this age group who were holding jobs, Townsend believed that this part of his plan would considerably reduce unemployment.

In 1939 101 members of the House of Representatives voted for the Townsend plan. This was not enough to make it law, but the vote demonstrates that the scheme had considerable backing. However, support for Townsend's plan decreased after his partner was found to have stolen the movement's funds.

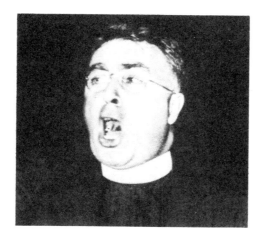

Charles Coughlin was a Catholic priest who influenced many people who listened to his radio broadcasts from Detroit. He accused Roosevelt of failing to keep his New Deal promises, of over-taxing the people, of being controlled by money-lenders, and of being a communist. After the 1936 election Father Coughlin's views became more extreme. He founded the Christian Front, an intolerant organisation which aimed to exterminate all Jews living in the United States.

Gerald Smith, Dr Townsend and Father Coughlin joined forces to oppose Franklin Roosevelt in the 1936 presidential election. They formed the Union Party and chose William Lemke as their candidate. The Republican Party's candidate was a popular and respected politician, Alfred Landon.

The result of the 1936 presidential election

Despite the opposition he faced, Franklin Roosevelt won the 1936 election easily. He received over 27 million votes, as opposed to less than 17 million for Landon and only 890,000 for Lemke – the largest majority of popular votes in American history. Roosevelt had expected to win, but not by such a large margin, so what explains his victory?

Firstly, his New Deal measures had helped millions of Americans directly. He was the man who had given them jobs, saved their homes, their farms, their savings. Despite the complaints of opponents that the New Deal was only possible because of 'soak the rich' taxes, Roosevelt's policies and his fireside chats explaining them convinced many voters that he was their friend.

Secondly, the assassination of Huey Long deprived the opposition of a leader who might have been even more attractive to the poor than Roosevelt was.

Finally, the Republican Party candidate, Alfred Landon, fought a lack-lustre campaign and failed to convince voters of the faults of the New Deal.

An analysis of voting patterns in the 1936 election shows that Roosevelt owed his victory to a new grouping of voters. His support had come mainly from farmers, labor unionists and the poor. Such voters were especially numerous in the industrial cities in the north, and the rural areas of the south and west. They included blacks, who in 1936 voted Democrat overwhelmingly for the first time.

Source 4A: A 1936 cartoon from the *Philadelphia Enquirer*, an anti-New Deal newspaper. Its caption was 'It's All Part of a Great Big Plan'.

THE TROJAN HORSE AT OUR GATE

Source 4B: A newspaper cartoon from the Chicago *Tribune*, September 1935.

1 Given below are four extracts from speeches made by Roosevelt's critics. Use the information on pages 40–41 to identify the speaker in each case. Quote one piece of evidence from each speech and explain how it suggests who the speaker is.

Speech 1

I propose that every big fortune shall be cut down immediately by a tax, to where no one will own more than a few million dollars.

I propose that the surplus of all the big fortunes shall go into United States ownership. In this way the government of the United States would come into possession of $165,000,000,000.

Then those with less than $5000 would be added to, so that every family would start life again with homestead possessions of at least the comforts needed for a home, including such things as a radio and an automobile.

Speech 2

It has become an accepted fact that because of man's inventiveness less and less productive effort is going to be required to supply the needs of the race. This being the case it is just as necessary to make some disposal of our surplus workers as it is to dispose of our surplus wheat or cotton. But we cannot kill off the surplus workers as we are doing with our hogs. We must retire them.

I suggest that the national government retire all who reach the age of sixty on a monthly pension of $200 on condition that they spend the money as they get it. This will ensure the even distribution throughout the nation of two or three billion dollars of fresh money each month.

Speech 3
No man in modern times received such plaudits [praise] from the poor as did Franklin Roosevelt when he promised to drive the money changers from the temple. March 4 1933! I shall never forget the inaugural address. The thrill that was mine was yours. Through the clouds of the Depression this man Roosevelt was a new saviour of his people.

My friends, what have we witnessed since then? The NRA which multiplied the profits of the monopolists [businessmen controlling trades or industries]. The AAA which raised the price of foodstuff.

In 1936 our disillusionment is complete. You citizens are saddled with a tax bill of $35,000,000,000 and your saviour's promises ring upon the counter of performance with the cheapness of tin.

Speech 4
I accept the nomination of the Republican Party for the Presidency of the United States. The time has come to stop fumbling with recovery. American initiative is not a commodity to be delivered in pound packages through a government bureau. It is a vital force in the life of our nation and it must be freed!.

2 Study the cartoons in Sources 4A and 4B. Use the information in this chapter to explain how each cartoon is critical of President Roosevelt.

3 a) List the similarities between the Long and Townsend plans.

b) Do you think any of Roosevelt's Second New Deal measures may have been influenced by Dr Townsend? Explain your answer.

4 a) List *three* of the criticisms being made of the New Deal at the time of the 1936 presidential election.

b) Suggest reasons why, despite the criticisms, Roosevelt had such an easy victory in the election.

The Supreme Court and the New Deal

Roosevelt and the New Deal also faced opposition from *inside* the American system of government.

The Federal (central) government of the United States has three sections: the executive, that is the president and his cabinet; the legislature, that is parliament, which is called Congress in America; and the judiciary, that is the law courts.

The highest law court in the United States is the Supreme Court which has the power of 'judicial review'. This means that it can decide whether particular laws meet conditions set out in the Constitution, the set of rules for running the country's government. So the Supreme Court can block the wishes of the president or Congress if its justices (judges) decide that those wishes are unconstitutional (not allowed by the Constitution).

In 1935 the Supreme Court checked the progress of the New Deal by declaring the National Recovery Administration (see page 24) unconstitutional. The reason given by the court was that the Constitution of the United States did not allow a president to make rules about how employers should treat their workers.

The court case which led to this decision involved a poultry firm called Schechter Brothers. They were accused of selling diseased chickens and not following the NRA regulations about workers' wages and hours of work. The Supreme Court ruled firstly that only Congress, not the president, could make regulations about working conditions, and secondly that the crime of selling diseased birds was the concern of the government of the state where the birds were sold, not the concern of the national government.

So the Schechters were acquitted and the affair became known as the 'sick-chicken case'. The contribution the NRA had made to the United States' economic recovery was at an end.

The Supreme Court continued to hinder the New Deal. In 1936 it also declared that the Agricultural Adjustment Act (see page 23) was unconstitutional. This time the court's reason was that regulations about agriculture should only be made by the individual states, not by the national government.

Source 4C: A 1936 cartoon from the *Washington Post*, a newspaper which usually supported Roosevelt. Its caption was 'The last of a Long Line'. The gravestones represent New Deal measures which have been declared unconstitutional by the Supreme Court.

Roosevelt hits back: the Court Packing Plan

President Roosevelt tried to stop the Supreme Court interfering with the New Deal by changing its membership. The Court had nine members, all appointed for life by the President. Roosevelt asked Congress to allow him to add six more, an extra justice for each one who refused to retire at the age of 70. In 1937, when Roosevelt suggested this, six of the nine justices were over 70. If his plan had been accepted the new judges would have supported the New Deal.

However, Congress rejected Roosevelt's plan by a large majority. Many members pointed out that the dictator Hitler had recently destroyed

45

democracy in Germany by tampering with the law courts and the rules of government. Some even accused Roosevelt himself of wanting to become a dictator.

Source 4D: A 1937 cartoon by J.N. Darling commenting on the Court Packing Plan.

The strength of the opposition to the court packing plan surprised Roosevelt. His proposals were not unconstitutional, for Congress had changed the number of Supreme Court justices several times in the past. However, many people did not realise this, and those who did still believed that allowing Roosevelt to interfere with the Supreme Court would make him too powerful.

Source 4E: A stamp produced by the Republican National Committee and used as a cartoon by the *Milwaukee Leader* on 16 January 1937.

Roosevelt's popularity was badly affected by his court plan. Years later David Kennedy, a banker with the Federal Reserve Board during the New Deal, described how it helped to change his opinion of the President:

> I was enthusiastic when Roosevelt came in. I thought: we're in serious trouble. Something has to be done, and here's a man that's going to do it. I voted for him for his first term and his second. After that, I voted against him. It wasn't just on the two-term basis, although that was important. The packing of the Supreme Court and the fact that we were not making the progress I thought our country was capable of making . . . I became terribly disenchanted.

Source 4F: From *Hard Times*, by Studs Terkel (1970).

The question of the composition of the Supreme Court also helped to divide the Democratic Party. Some conservative Democrats started voting with the Republicans in Congress against New Deal measures. This new anti-reform coalition was to remain a powerful political force until 1964.

Despite the failure of Roosevelt's scheme to pack the Supreme Court with his supporters, its justices had been shaken. Some retired voluntarily soon afterwards and the Court became less hostile to the New Deal. For example, when the Social Security Act (see page 28) and the Wagner Act (see page 31) came under judicial review later in 1937, both were accepted as being constitutional. In 1938 the Fair Labor Standards Act was passed, setting a minimum wage of 25 cents an hour and a maximum working week of 48 hours. This was just the sort of law that might well have been rejected by the Supreme Court before Roosevelt's attempt to reform it.

---

5 a) Name the three sections of the Federal government of the United States.

b) Explain how judicial review makes the Supreme Court a powerful part of the American government.

6 Look at Sources 4C, 4D and 4E.

a) What is the cartoonist suggesting is about to happen to the two men in Source 4C?

b) Explain the meaning of the words being spoken by the 'captain' in Source 4D.

c) Which cartoon do you think is more critical of Roosevelt and the New Deal? Explain your answer.

d) What 1937 event is being commented upon in Source 4E?

e) Are these sources expressing fact or opinion? Explain your answer.

7 Draw a cartoon which criticises *either* the Supreme Court as it was in 1936 *or* Roosevelt's plans to change it. Include a caption which makes your criticism clear.

The Recession of 1937–8

The New Deal was influenced by the theories of the British economist John Maynard Keynes. Keynes argued that a depression could be overcome by increased government spending on social services and public works. Such spending, he claimed, would put money into the economy and help it to revive. For example, a man employed in a government public works job would spend some of his wages on food for his family. This money would then be re-spent by the people who produced and sold the food, and so on.

Keynes said that the government should borrow money to finance its schemes if they cost more than the income it received from taxes. He believed that this 'deficit financing' (where a government's spending is greater than its income) was justified because it would place more people back in work and so lead to more spending and higher profits. The government would therefore be able to raise more money from taxes on people's incomes and profits, and thus repay the money it had borrowed.

However, in 1937 President Roosevelt tried to economise. He believed that the New Deal had helped the economy of the United States to recover sufficiently for him now to try to 'balance the budget', that is, to pay for public work schemes and make welfare payments out of the government's income, without borrowing.

Roosevelt's plan meant cutting back on various New Deal programmes. The money people earned and industrial production both fell as a result. Unemployment started to rise again. By early 1938, for example, one sixth of the population of New York City was on relief; in the city of Akron in Ohio the proportion was one third.

In April 1938 Congress made $4 billion available for the President to spend on Federal government recovery schemes. Nevertheless, it still hoped that Roosevelt would continue to try to balance the budget and was reluctant to give him all the money he wanted to continue the New Deal.

In an attempt to gain additional support for his ideas in Congress, in the 1938 Congressional elections Roosevelt spoke against the Democrats who opposed the New Deal. However, most of them were elected. So were eight new Republican senators and 81 new Republican Congressmen. As a result, although Roosevelt persuaded Congress to vote more money to help the unemployed of the northern industrial cities, he failed to persuade it to pass a single new New Deal law after 1938.

In his annual message to Congress in January 1939 Roosevelt promised that he would: 'invigorate the processes of recovery in order to preserve our reforms, and to give every man and woman who wants to work a real job and a living wage.'

But in fact, following the outbreak of war in Europe in 1939, the rest of Roosevelt's presidency was to be dominated by foreign affairs.

Source 4G: Two cartoons drawn by Daniel Fitzpatrick and published in the St Louis *Post-Dispatch* in 1938.

8 Look at Source 4G.

a) According to the cartoonist, what is the link between:

(i) the number of unemployed and the Federal government's budget (right)?
(ii) industrial production, unemployment and low wages (left)?

b) Do you think that the cartoonist is for, or against, the New Deal? Explain your answer.

The United States and the Second World War

An opinion poll conducted in 1937 showed that 95 per cent of Americans wanted the United States to keep out of any European war that might break out. In the same year half a million Americans signed a pledge not to support their government if it went to war.

Between 1935 and 1937 Congress passed a number of 'neutrality laws'. These aimed to keep the United States out of wars overseas by preventing American citizens from trading with countries which were at war, and from providing such countries with financial help.

In his speeches, including one he made during the election campaign of 1940, President Roosevelt himself promised repeatedly to keep the United States out of war. However, after the outbreak of the Second World War in 1939, Roosevelt believed that victory for the Axis (Germany, Italy and Japan) over the Allies (Britain, France, and, later the Soviet Union and China) might be followed by an attack on the United States. In a radio fireside chat, which he broadcast on 29 December 1940 he expressed these fears:

> If Great Britain goes down, the Axis powers will control the continents of Europe, Asia, Africa, Australia and the high seas – and they will be in a position to bring enormous military and naval resources against this hemisphere . . . There is far less chance of the United States getting into the war if we do all we can now to support the nations defending themselves against the Axis . . . We must be the arsenal of democracy.
> **Source 4H:** President Roosevelt, speaking to the American people on 29 December 1940.

Roosevelt devised several alternative ways to help the Allies, without actually declaring war on the Axis.

The Cash and Carry Deal, 1939

This allowed Britain and France to buy American arms and ammunition on condition that they paid in cash and transported the purchases in their own ships.

The Destroyer Transfer Agreement, 1940

By the summer of 1940 most of western Europe had been overrun by the armies of the German dictator, Hitler. Only Britain, exhausted and short of weapons, still defied them. Roosevelt decided to help by providing Britain with 50 American destroyers in exchange for being allowed to set up a number of American naval bases on British territories in the Atlantic and the Caribbean, for example in Newfoundland and British Guiana (now Guyana).

The Lend-Lease Act, 1941

By the end of 1940 Britain could no longer afford to buy war materials from the United States. But in March 1941 Congress approved a plan put forward by Roosevelt called 'Lend-Lease'. Lend-Lease allowed Roosevelt to 'transfer or lend' military equipment and other goods to Britain without immediate payment. He could do the same for any country whose defence he thought necessary to the safety of the USA. A great deal of Lend-Lease material was supplied to Chiang Kai Shek's Nationalist Chinese army, which was fighting the Japanese in eastern China.

The Atlantic Charter, 1941

This was an agreement drawn up by Roosevelt and the British Prime Minister Winston Churchill as a result of meetings in August 1941 on board the American cruiser *Augusta* and the British battleship *Prince of Wales*, off the coast of Newfoundland. The Charter pledged the United States and Britain to co-operate with each other to defeat the Axis – even though the United States was still not at war – and to continue to work together after the war had ended.

Opposition to Roosevelt's policies

The measures described above were unpopular with many Americans for two reasons. Firstly, despite Roosevelt's warnings, they believed that the Atlantic and Pacific oceans would keep the United States safe from attack even if Germany, Italy and Japan conquered the whole of Europe and Asia. By taking sides against the Axis, they believed that Roosevelt was putting American lives and the safety of the United States at risk. Secondly, they wanted Roosevelt to concentrate on overcoming the Depression.

The poster in source 4I and the cartoon in Source 4J sum up the way many Americans felt about the Second World War before 1941.

Source 4I: A poster issued by the America First Committee.

Source 4J: A cartoon drawn by Daniel Fitzpatrick and published in the St Louis *Post Dispatch*.

Support for opinions like these caused Roosevelt to explain repeatedly how the defence of the United States was being served by aiding the Allies instead of remaining neutral. His most famous speech on this subject came to be called the 'Four Freedoms' speech. In this speech he tried to show why it was necessary to help the Allies, both to defend freedom everywhere and to defend the achievements of the New Deal in the United States:

> The basic things expected by our people of their political and economic systems are simple. They are:
> Equality of opportunity for youth and others.
> Jobs for those who can work.
> Security for those who need it.
> The ending of special privilege for the few.
> The preservation of civil liberties for all.
> The enjoyment of the fruits of scientific progress in a wider and constantly rising standard of living.
>
> In the future days which we seek to make secure, we look forward to a world founded upon four essential human freedoms. The first is freedom of speech and expression – everywhere in the world.
>
> The second is freedom of every person to worship God in his own way – everywhere in the world.
>
> The third is freedom from want – which, translated into world terms, means economic understandings which will secure to every nation a healthy peacetime life for its inhabitants – everywhere in the world.
>
> The fourth is freedom from fear, which, translated into world terms, means a world-wide reduction of armaments to such a point and in such a thorough manner that no nation will be in a position to commit an act of physical aggression against any neighbour – anywhere in the world.
>
> Our support goes to those who struggle to gain those rights and keep them. Our strength is in our unity of purpose.
> **Source 4K:** From a speech made by Franklin Roosevelt on 6 January 1941.

Despite the President's 'Four Freedoms' speech, many Americans still did not want their country to become involved in the war. For example, a group called The America First Committee wrote to Roosevelt to express its concern on 6 December 1941:

> Dear Mr. President,
> What is all this sabre rattling in connection with Japan? Why are our sons wanted to fight a war 10,000 miles away – must we close our eyes to our urgent domestic problems?
> **Source 4L:** From a letter to President Roosevelt from the America First Committee.

The United States goes to war

The day after the letter quoted above was written Japanese planes attacked Pearl Harbor, an American naval base in the Hawaiian Islands. Over 3000 American servicemen and civilians were killed or wounded and eight battleships were destroyed. Roosevelt asked Congress to declare war on Japan.

On 8 December The America First Committee wrote to the President again:

> Dear Mr. President,
> In view of the fact that we are now at war with Japan, please consider the contents of our letter, dated 6th December 1941, null and void.
> We stand behind you in your endeavour to win this war. We pledge you our support.
> **Source 4M:** From a letter to President Roosevelt from the America First Committee.

But some Americans continued to blame Roosevelt for involving the United States in the war:

In the 1940 campaign he [Roosevelt] made a pledge to mothers and fathers that their sons would not be sent to fight in any foreign wars. It was absolutely a dishonest, dishonourable, contemptible statement, because he had been planning to get us in all the time . . . There were three reasons why Roosevelt wanted war. One: you had ten million Americans unemployed after six years of the New Deal. The other one: to be a war President, you became a great man overnight. And then, he hoped to put through a United Nations, of which he would be the author – and the uncrowned ruler of the world.

Source 4N: From an interview given by Hamilton Fish, a Republican Congressman, in the 1960s. In *Hard Times*, by Studs Terkel (1970).

Four days after the Pearl Harbor attack Japan's allies, Germany and Italy, declared war on the United States. Between 1941 and 1945 the American economy was transformed as production was stepped up to make the goods needed to defeat the Axis.

The United States armed forces employed 15 million people during the war years, of whom 7 million were combat troops. Many of these had been unemployed in the 1930s, as had many of the 6 million extra civilians who were employed to manufacture weapons. By the end of the war these industrial workers had produced 297,000 planes, 86,000 tanks, 6,500 naval vessels, 64,500 landing craft, 17 million rifles and 4.2 million tons of artillery shells. As Roosevelt had promised, the United States had indeed become the 'arsenal of democracy'.

Sources 4O and 4P give an impression of how the United States' entry into the war transformed the lives of ordinary people:

The war boom brought unprecedented prosperity to millions. Thanks largely to time-and-a-half payment for overtime work, weekly earnings in manufacturing rose 70%. The Okies, the migratory farm workers who had been pariahs [outcasts] during the '30s, found themselves welcomed at employment offices. Domestics left the pantry for the assembly line. Men who had been jobless for years found themselves making $100 a week and better. Many seized on the war prosperity to buy their way out of debt. In 1944 a woman in a Kansas City bakery started a great row when she blurted out: 'I hope the war lasts a long time so we can pay off our mortgage.'

Source 4O: From *The New Deal and War*, by W.E. Leuchtenburg (1964).

I'd rather be in the army than outside where I was so raggedy and didn't have no jobs. I was glad to put on a United States Army uniform and get some food. I'd rather be in the army now than see another Depression.

Source 4P: From an interview given by Louis Banks, a washroom attendant, in the 1960s. In *Hard Times*, by Studs Terkel (1970).

The Second World War helped to establish some of the New Deal ideas that Roosevelt had originally found difficult to introduce. For example, the National Recovery Administration and Wagner Act regulations intended to prevent disputes between workers and employers, which had been difficult to enforce in the 1930s, now worked well. Union membership increased, reaching 15 million by 1945, and there were very few strikes.

On the other hand, other New Deal measures were attacked by Roosevelt's opponents during the war. In the 1942 Congressional elections the Republicans won nine extra senate seats and 46 extra seats in the House of Representatives. They used this new strength to bring the National Youth Administration (see page 30) and the Farm Security Administration (see page 35) to an end. They also blocked Roosevelt's proposal to expand the provision of social security after the war had ended.

Roosevelt accepted that there would be few opportunities for further reforms until the Axis was defeated. 'Dr New Deal must give way to Dr Win-the-War', he said.

However, after his fourth presidential election victory in 1944 Roosevelt began planning to revive the New Deal. Henry Wallace, a strong New Deal supporter, was appointed Secretary of Commerce, and legislation to provide better health care, education and social insurance was prepared.

But on 12 April 1945 Roosevelt died of a stroke. The President's sudden death prevented his plans to revive the New Deal from becoming law. After the war ended later that year, Harry Truman, Roosevelt's successor as President of the United States, introduced his own ideas for relief and reform. Truman called his programme 'The Fair Deal'.

The Fair Deal did not need to help the Amerian economy to recover; the war had achieved this and fewer than 1 million people were now unemployed. However, it did try to build on the New Deal relief and reform measures, especially for the benefit of the poor.

---

9 Look at Source 4J.

a) What message is the cartoonist trying to give the readers of the St Louis *Post-Dispatch*?

b) Use the information in Sources 4K, 4O and 4P to write a letter to the editor of the newspaper. You should complain about Fitzpatrick's cartoon and point out the possible advantages of American entry into the Second World War.

10 a) Identify by letter the sources in this section which oppose American entry into the Second World War.

b) List the reasons for remaining neutral that are given in these sources.

11 Look at Source 4N.

a) According to Hamilton Fish, why did Roosevelt want to involve the United States in the Second World War?

b) Pick out from Fish's interview (i) two statements of fact and (ii) two statements of opinion.

c) Imagine you are someone who supported Roosevelt's policies in 1940 and 1941. Write a reply to Fish's claims about the President.

Assessments of the New Deal

The forgotten man is still forgotten. The New Deal has only helped big business.

President Roosevelt is certainly a Saviour to the Country.
(Two judgements of the New Deal made in letters sent to President Roosevelt in 1934 and 1935.)

What was distinctive about the New Deal?

The 1930s was not the only period during which the United States experienced an economic depression. But the depression which occurred at that time is particularly important because it was the worst in American history and because of the way President Roosevelt tackled it – with the New Deal.

Several features of the New Deal make it distinctive:

1 The New Deal was the first time that the Federal government had accepted responsibility for the nation's poor. Previously, dealing with poverty had been left to charities and to the individual states, with the national government playing only a supporting role. The New Deal is therefore a landmark in American history because the national government took the lead in trying to provide solutions to the problems caused by the Depression.

2 The New Deal was a sustained experiment that included many features like social security which were entirely new in the American experience. President Roosevelt was prepared to try new and sometimes unpopular methods if they seemed likely to provide relief or assist economic recovery.

3 The New Deal enabled organised labour to become a powerful political force in the United States for the first time. Earlier in the twentieth century labor unions had faced the opposition of the government as well as that of the employers, and had experienced little success. After the Wagner Act there was a great increase in union membership, and fair practice contracts were frequently negotiated with employers or forced out of them by strikes. The support of labor unions became an important factor in the electoral success of Democratic politicians.

4 The New Deal still influences the way American governments try to deal with poverty. Although the New Deal itself ended at the time of the Second World War, some of its features can still be recognised in the United States today.

The social welfare programme first introduced by the Social Security Act in 1935 was vastly expanded in the 1960s, after the collapse of the anti-reform coalition formed by conservative Republicans and Democrats towards the end of the New Deal. For example, in 1965 national health insurance for the old, known as 'Medicare' and for the poor, known as 'Medicaid' was introduced.

Since the New Deal local and voluntary solutions to poverty have remained less important than government initiatives, despite several attempts to cut back on welfare spending by the Federal government.

Most Americans are now part of the national social security system which began during the New Deal, even if it is only in their eventual capacity as old age pensioners.

5 The New Deal changed the way people thought about the role of government in their individual lives. After the New Deal most Americans were prepared to accept government regulation of business and industry, as well as its involvement in the organisation of social welfare schemes.

6 The New Deal also altered the way the American government itself was organised. Changes were introduced to enable the government to cope with its extra responsibilities; for example, the Executive Office was created to help the president to carry out his job. Amongst other things, these changes resulted in vast increases in the number of people employed by the Federal government.

What did the New Deal do for blacks and women?

Blacks

It is perhaps difficult to understand why blacks supported Roosevelt in the 1936 election. In 1932 most black votes had gone to the Republicans and Roosevelt had done little in the interim to improve the position of blacks in American society. They remained second-class citizens, suffering humiliating discrimination in services such as restaurants, cinemas, education and public transport, as can be seen from the photograph in Source 5A.

Source 5A: A segregated beach in the 1930s.

Prejudice and racism were widespread. Lynch mobs murdered 63 blacks between 1933 and 1935. In terms of employment, the 1940 census showed that whilst one in three whites had desk jobs, only one in 20 blacks did. Only one in ten white women who worked was employed as a maid, whereas six out of ten working black women did this low-status job. Some New Deal schemes perpetuated segregation. For instance, there were separate black and white CCC camps, and blacks were not allowed to live in Norris, a new town built as part of the Tennessee Valley Authority programme.

Roosevelt claimed that he wanted to help blacks more, but could not do so for fear of upsetting southern white congressmen. If this group stopped supporting his New Deal plans, he argued, the blacks who benefited from them would be in an even worse position. The Depression hit the black population hard. A total of 30 per cent were on relief in 1935.

However, Clifford Burke, a black himself, claimed that blacks were able to cope with the Depression better than whites:

The negro was born in depression. It didn't mean much to him. The Great Depression as you call it. There was no such thing. The best he could be was a janitor or porter or shoeshine boy. It only became official when it hit the white man.

Source 5B: From an interview in the 1960s. In *Hard Times,* by Studs Terkel (1970).

But although blacks benefited less than whites from the New Deal, they still benefited. Those living in northern cities were able to obtain relief on similar terms to whites. Even in the southern states, where anti-black racism was at its strongest, the New Deal gave poor blacks far more aid than they had ever received before. Many came to feel that their survival depended on the New Deal's relief cheques and that a vote for Roosevelt was their best hope for an improvement in their position in the future.

Women

Women played a significant role in shaping the New Deal. Frances Perkins, an important member of FDR's cabinet and a supporter of social security (see page 17), and Eleanor Roosevelt, the President's wife, were particularly important. The two women built up a network of other talented women, especially ones with experience in welfare work. The expertise and know-how of these women proved invaluable in working out and putting into practice many of the New Deal's social reforms. The Works Progress Administration (see page 29), for example, called upon their help for the development of projects specifically aimed at women.

Many Americans preferred to write to Mrs Roosevelt about their problems rather than to the President himself. Most of them were women asking for clothing or money. This was considered a more acceptable thing for women than men to do at the time, In making such requests, women were seen as simply trying to help their families. If men had done so it would have been viewed as a humiliating admission that they were unable to provide for their dependents.

In the 1930s the American work force was mainly male, and New Deal measures such as the Civilian Conservation Corps and the National Youth Administration helped men rather than women. The provision of aid for women and their dependent children by the Social Security Act was one of the few parts of the New Deal which set out to help women specifically. Even then, some states tried to avoid paying it where possible; for example this type of assistance was often given only to mothers who had no illegitimate children.

Was the New Deal successful?

People who lived through the Depression held different opinions about the New Deal. Some Americans, like Huey Long and Father Coughlin, hated it passionately, and some historians, while trying to judge the period more objectively, claim that the Depression would have continued if the Second World War had not revived the American economy.

One person who thought this at the time was the British journalist Malcolm Muggeridge. Writing in 1940 he claimed that 'derelict factories and shipyards continued idle until war spurred them into renewed activity; in peace they were paralysed'.

Yet Roosevelt was a popular president who was elected with large majorities on four occasions, which suggests that many Americans must have believed that the New Deal was working. Some historians agree with this opinion. Daniel Snowman, for example, wrote the following:

> Roosevelt's administration did much to alleviate [relieve] the unprecedented suffering with which the country was faced . . . The administration also took a number of significant steps to try to ensure that, once the Depression was ended, there could never be another of similar proportions.

Source 5C: From *America Since 1920,* by Daniel Snowman (1968).

However, opinion needs to be based on evidence. Earlier sections of this book contain numerous examples of both opinion and evidence concerning the New Deal. Together with the following collection, they should help you to form your own views about the answer to the question 'Was the New Deal successful?'

Evidence and opinions

The New Deal is nothing more or less than an effort by an inexperienced demagogue [a leader whose popularity is based on lies] to take away from the thrifty what they and their ancestors have accumulated, and give it to others who have not earned it, and thus destroy the incentive for all future accumulation.

Source 5D: Adapted from a pamphlet published by the American Liberty League, which supported Landon in the 1936 election.

Year	Unemployed (in millions)	Unemployed (% of workforce)	Millions employed by Federal government (1933–42)
1929	1.5	3.2	
1930	4.3	8.7	
1931	8.0	15.9	
1932	12.1	23.6	
1933	12.8	24.9	4.3
1934	11.3	21.7	1.1
1935	10.6	20.1	4.0
1936	9.0	16.9	3.8
1937	7.7	14.3	2.7
1938	10.4	19.0	4.3
1939	9.5	17.2	3.3
1940	8.1	14.6	2.9
1941	5.6	9.9	1.8
1942	2.6	4.7	0.4
1943	1.8	2.3	
1944	1.0	1.2	

(Presidential election years are indicated by the use of italics.)

Source 5E

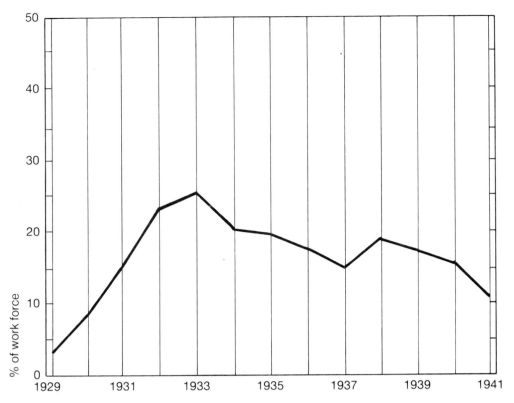

Source 5F: Unemployment in the United States 1929–41.

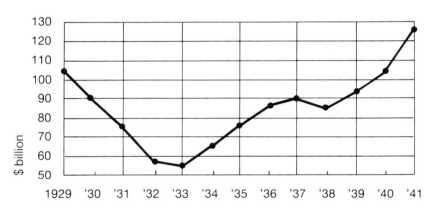

Source 5G: National Income in the United States 1929–41. (National Income – also called Gross National Product – is calculated by adding together the values of all the goods (steel, cars, clothing etc.) and all the services (catering, transport etc.) produced in one year.)

Labor gained more under President Roosevelt than any president in memory.
Source 5H: John L. Lewis, leader of the United Mine Workers, speaking on behalf of Roosevelt in the 1936 presidential election campaign.

Economic revival in the United States dates from the outbreak of war in Europe in September, 1939 . . . It was like watching blood drain back into a blanched face of a person who had fainted.
Source 5I: Broadus Mitchell's view of the effect of the Second World War on the American economy, from *Depression Decade* (1947).

Source 5J: Two photographs of sandwich-board boys advertising Roosevelt's New Deal achievements.

Roosevelt forged a new political coalition [alliance] based on the masses in the great northern cities. It won the allegiance of a diverse group of leaders who not only supported Roosevelt's national social reforms but inaugurated 'little New Deals' in their own states.

Source 5K: Adapted from William Leuchtenburg, writing in *New Deal and War* (1964).

Consider what the seemingly piecemeal struggles of these six years add up to in terms of realistic national preparedness.

We are conserving and developing natural resources – land, water, power, forests.

We are trying to provide necessary food, shelter and medical care for the health of our population.

We are putting agriculture – our system of food and fiber supply – on a sounder basis.

We are strengthening the weakest spot in our system of industrial supply – its long smouldering labor difficulties.

We have cleaned up our credit system so that depositer and investor alike may more readily and willingly make their capital available for peace or war.

We are giving to our youth new opportunities for work and education.

We have sustained the morale of all the population by the dignified recognition of our obligations to the aged, the helpless and the needy.

Source 5L: From President Roosevelt's message to Congress, 4 January 1939.

The legacy of the New Deal was in ideas and attitudes. These years brought a revolution in the thinking of the American people about the place of the Federal government in their lives. Roosevelt's work persuaded them to accept it as a positive source of social welfare, in a way which would have been unthinkable before 1933. The great reforms – the regulation of banking, the limitation upon hours of work – have remained part of the American social fabric, unchanged even in the years of Republican rule in the 1950s.

Further, the New Deal – as Americans were not slow to realize – was an episode of international importance. It was a democratic and peaceful revolution, the achievement of a free people, whose voters put Franklin Roosevelt into power and freely confirmed him in office, at a time when so much of contemporary Europe was being dragooned and deceived into submission by the dictators Hitler, Mussolini and Stalin. And it was not the least of Roosevelt's achievements that he gave a new heart and new vigour to his fellow-countrymen just in time to face the trial of the Second World War.

Source 5M: From *The USA Since the First World War*, by C. P. Hill (1967).

Roosevelt, with his silver tongue, brought words of hope. He started many things going, but they were turned on and off. We had the NRA and WPA and these things – they'd come and go. You never could get clear cut decisions. One day, one thing; the next day another. It was bedlam and confusion in Washington.

Source 5N: From an interview given by David Kennedy in the 1960s. In *Hard Times*, by Studs Terkel (1970).

When Congress adjourned on June 16 [1933], precisely one hundred days after the special session opened, it had written into the laws of the land the most extraordinary series of reforms in the nation's history. It had committed the country to an unprecedented program of government – industry co-operation; promised to distribute stupendous sums to millions of staple farmers; accepted responsibility for the welfare of millions of unemployed; agreed to engage in far-reaching experimentation in regional planning; pledged billions of dollars to save homes and farms from foreclosure; undertaken huge public works spending; guaranteed the small bank deposits of the country; and had, for the first time, established federal regulation of Wall Street.

The next day, as the president sat at his desk in the White House signing several of the bills Congress had adopted, including the largest peacetime appropriation bill ever passed, he remarked. 'More history is being made today than in [any] one day of our national life.' Oklahoma's Senator Thomas Gore amended: 'During all time.'

Source 5O: From *Franklin Roosevelt and the New Deal*, by W.E. Leuchtenburg (1964).

Use the sources in the section 'Evidence and opinions' to answer these questions.

1 Identify by letter all the sources which are examples of:

a) evidence about the New Deal;

b) opinion about the New Deal.

2 Identify by letter the sources which suggest that:

a) the New Deal was a success;

b) the New Deal was a failure.

c) What reasons are given by the sources listed in b) for believing the New Deal was a failure?

3 Identify by letter all the sources which are examples of:

a) primary information;

b) secondary information.

4 Look at Source 5E.

a) By how many millions was unemployment reduced during the New Deal years 1933–40?

b) According to the statistics provided in this source, what was one reason for this reduction?

5 Look at Sources 5F and 5G.

a) At the end of which year:

(i) did unemployment reach its peak?
(ii) had there been the greatest increase in national income?

b) Which events mentioned in this chapter explain why:

(i) the unemployment graph line rises between 1937 and 1938?
(ii) the national income graph line rises between 1940 and 1941?

6 Compare Source 5E with Source 5J. In which year is it most likely that the photographs were taken? Explain your answer.

7 Look at Source 5L. Use other sections in the book to name the New Deal measure President Roosevelt is referring to in the following statements:

a) 'We are conserving and developing natural resources . . .'

b) 'We are putting agriculture . . . on a sounder basis.'

c) 'We are strengthening the weakest spot in our system of industrial supply . . .'

d) 'We have sustained . . . the helpless and the needy.'

8 Look at Source 5O. Is W.E. Leuchtenburg simply recording facts, expressing an opinion, or both? Write down words or phrases from the extract to support your answer.

9 From the information you have collected for question 8 and the sources you have identified in your answer to question 2, write an essay arguing that the New Deal was *either* a success *or* a failure.